THE CRITICS DEBATE

General Editor: Michael Scott

The Critics Debate
General Editor: Michael Scott
Published titles:
Sons and Lovers Geoffrey Harvey
Bleak House Jeremy Hawthorn
The Canterbury Tales Alcuin Blamires
Tess of the d'Urbervilles Terence Wright
Hamlet Michael Hattaway
The Waste Land and Ash Wednesday
   Arnold P. Hinchliffe
Paradise Lost Margarita Stocker
King Lear Ann Thompson
Othello Peter Davison

Further titles are in preparation.

OTHELLO

Peter Davison

MACMILLAN

First published 1988

Published by
Higher and Further Education Division
MACMILLAN PUBLISHERS LTD
Houndmills, Basingstoke, Hampshire RG21 2XS
and London
Companies and representatives
throughout the world

Typeset by Wessex Typesetters
(Division of The Eastern Press Ltd)
Frome, Somerset

Printed in Hong Kong

British Library Cataloguing in Publication Data
Davison, P. H.
    Othello.——(The Critics debate).
    1. Shakespeare, William. Othello
    I. Title II. Series
    822.3'3   PR2829
ISBN 0-333-38694-9
ISBN 0-333-38695-7 Pbk

5

Contents

General Editor's Preface   6
A Note on Text and References   7

Introduction   9

Part One: Survey   15

Genre criticism   15
Historical and social criticism   20
Dramatic convention and decorum   27
Character and psychological criticism   34
The play as dramatic poem   44
Archetypal criticism   51

Part Two: Appraisal   59

Contextual criticism   59
  The text   61
  Racial difference   62
  Character antithesis   67
  Othello and tragic error   77
  Double time and its implications   79

Further Reading and References   86
Index   93

General Editor's Preface

OVER THE last few years the practice of literary criticism has become hotly debated. Methods developed earlier in the century and before have been attacked and the word 'crisis' has been drawn upon to describe the present condition of English Studies. That such a debate is taking place is a sign of the subject discipline's health. Some would hold that the situation necessitates a radical alternative approach which naturally implies a 'crisis situation'. Others would respond that to employ such terms is to precipitate or construct a false position. The debate continues but it is not the first. 'New Criticism' acquired its title because it attempted something fresh, calling into question certain practices of the past. Yet the practices it attacked were not entirely lost or negated by the new critics. One factor becomes clear: English Studies is a pluralistic discipline.

What are students coming to advanced work in English for the first time to make of all this debate and controversy? They are in danger of being overwhelmed by the cross-currents of critical approaches as they take up their study of literature. The purpose of this series is to help delineate various critical approaches to specific literary texts. Its authors are from a variety of critical schools and have approached their task in a flexible manner. Their aim is to help the reader come to terms with the variety of criticism and to introduce him or her to further reading on the subject and to a fuller evaluation of a particular text by illustrating the way it has been approached in a number of contexts. In the first part of the book a critical survey is given of some of the major ways the text has been appraised. This is done sometimes in a thematic manner, sometimes according to various 'schools' or 'approaches'. In the second part the authors provide their own appraisals of the text from their stated critical standpoint, allowing the reader the knowledge of their own particular approaches from which their views may in turn be evaluated. The series therein hopes to introduce and to elucidate criticism of authors and texts being studied and to encourage participation as the critics debate.

Michael Scott

A Note on Text and References

ALL quotations from *Othello* are from the New Cambridge edition, edited by Norman Sanders (Cambridge, 1984), and the few quotations from Shakespeare's other works are taken from *William Shakespeare: The Complete Works*, edited by Peter Alexander (London and Glasgow, 1951). The line references supplied (usually in *square* brackets, though sometimes in the main text) relate to these editions. Act and scene are included in the reference except where there is continued reference to the same scene.

With a few exceptions the other sources cited are given in the section 'Further Reading and References'. Most of these sources are identified in the text by author and date of publication of the edition cited, using which information they can be readily traced in the alphabetical list of references at the end of the 'Further Reading' section. Two important collections of criticism are identified by abbreviation:

C – the Macmillan *Casebook* on *Othello* (London, 1971)
ShS 21 – *Shakespeare Survey 21* (Cambridge, 1970)

Details of the criticism included in *C* (which is cited wherever it includes the relevant passage) and *ShS 21* are given preceding the alphabetical list of references. *All* page references – with date or abbreviation except where there is continued reference to the same source (or, in the case of *C* and *ShS 21*, the same *item*) – appear in *round* brackets.

For Martha

Introduction

The end of reading or listening is the beginning
of critical understanding.
(Northrop Frye, 1963, p. 61)

Shakespeare's compositions, from the very depth
of purpose displayed in them, have been exposed
to the misfortune of being misunderstood
(Schlegel, 1840, ii, 130)

IT IS a commonplace that critics find very different things to
admire and condemn in great works of literature – even as to
whether they are great. As the great German author and critic,
Schlegel (1767–1845), pointed out nearly two hundred years
ago, Shakespeare's 'very depth of purpose' has caused him to
be particularly subject to misinterpretation. Shakespeare, said
Lessing (1729–81), whom Schlegel quoted,

> gives a living picture of all the most minute and secret
> artifices by which a feeling steals into our souls, of all the
> imperceptible advantages which it there gains, of all the
> stratagems by which every other passion is made subservient
> to it, till it becomes the sole tyrant of our desires and our
> aversions.   (1840, ii, 137)

Although Lessing, mainstay of the Enlightenment in Germany,
was writing in general terms of Shakespeare, what he says has
peculiar force for *Othello* and its hero. In the theatre, in even a
half-way decent production, the play is, in Bradley's words,
'most painfully exciting and most terrible'. But, having
listened, having, as audience, participated in the performance,
we are only at the threshold of critical understanding. Literary
criticism, according to Northrop Frye, is too often based on
value-judgements given credence by fashion (see conclusion to
'Archetypal criticism' in Part One below), and what was so
effective in the theatre is sometimes regarded in the study as a
rather hollow achievement. Even one of the most
understanding of critics, whilst acknowledging *Othello*'s 'great
theatrical power', finds 'a certain thinness in its imaginative

rhetoric' (Emrys Jones, 1971, p. 117). Thomas Rymer, nearly three hundred years ago, was particularly harsh on the tragic pretensions of *Othello*. It was, he complained, 'none other than a Bloody Farce, without salt or savour' (*C*, p. 48). Shakespeare, he says, 'against all Justice and Reason, against Law, Humanity, and Nature, in a barbarous, arbitrary way, executes and makes havock of his subjects, *Hab-nab*, as they come to hand' (p. 46). This is critical, certainly, but hardly that critical *understanding* to which Northrop Frye would have us aspire.

No one will be surprised to find critics at variance, whether they are scholarly or journalistic. We are accustomed to wondering whether newspaper critics have attended the same opening nights, so diverse can be their responses. What is surprising, perhaps, is the degree of acrimony, *personal* acrimony, betrayed by some critics towards one another or even towards Othello, in their discussions of this play. In a subject laying claim to being a humane discipline, this is odd, even disturbing. F. R. Leavis's denigration of A. C. Bradley's interpretation of Othello is little more savage and contemptuous than his criticism of Othello, to whom he compares him. Bradley's account of Othello's jealousy, says Dr Leavis, 'is as extraordinary a history of triumphant sentimental perversity as literary history can show' (*C*, p. 126); and, having commented upon 'Othello's noble lack of self-knowledge' being 'shown as humiliating and disastrous' (p. 135), he first equates Bradley's knowledge of Othello with Othello's of himself – i.e. totally lacking – and then has a second bite at this cherry, 'to equate Bradley's knowledge of Othello with Othello's own was perhaps unfair to Othello' (p. 136).

Leavis is not alone in flagellating rival critics. Elmer Stoll remarked, 'If Mr Clutton Brock cannot and will not read Shakespeare's score [of *Othello*], Mr [Wilson] Knight cannot and will not read the text. He reads the letters only . . .' (1933, p. 3). We may feel we are not so much in a debate about *Othello* as in a battle. Yet, apart from a few excesses and inconsistencies, it is notable how much of the criticism of this play is convincing *in its own terms*. It is easy to maintain that a drama-as-a-poem critic is misinterpreting a play by ignoring flesh-and-blood stage presentation, but such criticism, well founded, can illuminate not only the poetry but also the drama.

Perhaps a measure of *Othello*'s qualities is that it can simultaneously admit of views as opposed as those of Maud Bodkin and Dame Helen Gardner, S. L. Bethell and Wilson Knight, and even Bradley and Leavis.

Nevertheless, the student cannot simply accept at face value what critics say. There are errors and inconsistencies which have to be taken into account even if one is willing to accept a critic on his or her own terms. Take the relatively simple matter of Shakespeare's source-story. Harley Granville-Barker wrote, 'Cinthio's is a convincing story; its characters are clearly drawn, and it is in its spare fashion, very well told' (1963, p. 135). G. M. Matthews sees Cinthio's story differently: 'Shakespeare had no need to borrow Cinthio's original story if all he wanted was a tragedy of jealous love; it is not a very good story, and nobody in the [original] audience would have known it except a few highbrows who read Italian' (1975, p. 110). Quite apart from the different value-judgements placed on the story, those who read French – many more than those able to read Italian – could have known the story, for it had been translated into French and published in England in 1584.

Such discrepancies point to the need for every reader to exercise his or her own critical judgements. Criticism, like any other form of communication should not be taken at face value: it must be, as Shakespeare wrote in another context, 'deep searched'. Conflicting assessments of *Othello*, and the acrimony exhibited by some critics, may be explained by a fundamental misunderstanding about the play.

The story is quite simple, whether or not Cinthio told it well. It seems open, therefore, if not to 'simple' approaches, then to single-minded attack. However, as John Bayley acutely demonstrates, *Othello* is not 'a simple clear-cut affair' which demands of the critic no more than a working-out of 'what kind of simplicity' is being dramatised. The play, he argues, is a 'highly complex affair': it is 'a tragedy of incomprehension . . . at the very deepest level of human dealings'. Far from it being a matter of Bradley's lack of self-knowledge (as Leavis puts it), 'No one in *Othello* comes to understand himself or anyone else. None of them realise their situation' (*C*, p. 169). Furthermore, he argues, in *Othello* we do not have 'mutually inclusive "meanings"' but have 'successive and at first mutually exclusive points of view' (p. 171).

If Professor Bayley is right, we need to be careful not to try to dig out some over-simplified 'meaning' for the play, Othello, Iago, or Desdemona, but instead be prepared to respond simultaneously to aspects that might seem contradictory and even irrational. Pursuing a particular line of approach single-mindedly, seeing Othello in some hard-cast form, or Iago as having a sharply defined nature of a particular kind or conventional form and no more, may reveal interesting *aspects* of the play, but can do so at the expense of distorting the whole. And the whole of *Othello* depends upon contradiction, irrationality and complexity, 'simple' tale though it is. Perhaps no other element demonstrates this than the play's famous – or infamous – 'double time scheme'. As it stands, looked at rationally, and disregarding a few niceties, the story of Othello and Desdemona as told in the last four acts of the play couldn't have happened: time did not allow. Yet, we 'witness' it all happen and are moved by what we see. Scholars may explain how double time arose, as Ned B. Allen has done, arguing that Shakespeare wrote Acts I and II at a different time from Acts III–v, then 'splic[ed] together two parts not originally written to go together' (*ShS 21*, p. 24). It is often said that double time doesn't matter because in the theatre we don't notice. But Shakespeare and his company can scarcely not have noticed, so perhaps the significant question is, 'Why does Shakespeare make his plot depend upon so irrational a time plan?'

Norman Sanders, in his Introduction to the New Cambridge edition of the play, remarks that, though there are plenty of illuminating analyses of aspects of *Othello*, there is no consensus about the nature of the unique world of the play. It is curious too, he says, that completely satisfying productions can have at their heart very different readings of Othello and his nature.

If inconsistency and incomprehension are at the core of *Othello*, then it will not be surprising if one of Shakespeare's ways of dramatising his story and those who enact it is a two- or three-way, mutually exclusive, representation of characters and events. His genius is to encompass such contradictions within a convincing whole. Thus, we can see Desdemona as simple innocent and as wilful, knowing, disobedient daughter; Iago as malevolent, scheming character, as innate Evil personified, and as dramatic stereotype; and the milieu as domestic 'reality' and as world of wonder. It is not surprising, then, that Othello's complexity should lead to his being interpreted variously as not easily jealous, as jealous by nature, and as too readily deceived by a simple device so that he becomes passionately jealous. But are we being deceived as easily as Othello?

Before surveying a number of critical approaches, two general points might be offered. First a remark by J. I. M. Stewart about reading criticism: 'The lesson is surely not that all critical interpretation of Shakespeare's characters is ephemeral modish nonsense. We merely learn that we ought not to let one theory, one reading, sweep all others away' (1963, p. 299). Secondly, a more troubling warning from Susan Sontag's essay 'Against Interpretation':

In most modern instances, interpretation amounts to the philistine refusal to leave the work of art alone. Real art has the capacity to make us nervous. By reducing the work of art to its content and then interpreting *that*, one tames the work of art. Interpretation makes art manageable, conformable.

In the edition before me in which this essay is collected (1969, p. 17), 'conformable' is spelt 'comformable'; in David Lodge's *20th Century Literary Criticism* the word has become 'comfortable' (1972, p. 656). What is certain is that *Othello* is *not* a comfortable play: neither is its style, its construction, or its matter conformable; and it ought to make us uneasy, even a little nervous.

Part One
Survey

*There is no such thing as Shakespearian Tragedy:
there are only Shakespearian tragedies.*
(Kenneth Muir, 1972, p. 12)

Genre criticism

AS A critical approach, 'Genre' may seem distinctly odd,
especially for the plays of Shakespeare. Were they not, from the
very first collected edition, classified as comedies, histories and
tragedies? Yes, of course – but within that neat pigeon-holing
lurk inconsistencies. Histories may also be described in their
first editions as tragedies – *Richard II* is an example; *Cymbeline*
and *The Winter's Tale*, which are often categorised as 'romances'
or even as 'last plays', were quite differently 'placed' in the first
edition of Shakespeare's complete works, the former among the
tragedies and the latter among the comedies. And *Troilus and
Cressida* was styled a tragedy in the First Folio of 1623, a history
on the title-page of the 1609 quarto, and discussed in a preface
to the latter as if it were a comedy!

It is easy to think such classifications are no more than a
minor pedantic puzzle, but our attitude to a work may be much
conditioned by how it is described. More important, an
understanding of genre may give insight into what is going on
in a work of art. For example, is what we read to be taken at face
value or is the author being ironic? This is obvious in discussion
of *Troilus and Cressida*. It is less obvious, but perhaps even more
significant, for *Othello*.

Thomas Rymer was prepared to dismiss the notion that
Othello had any claim to be called a tragedy. It had 'some
burlesk, humour and ramble of Comical Wit . . . but the
tragical part is plainly none other than a Bloody Farce' (*C*,
p. 48). What he found deficient in *Othello*, which he saw from
the standpoint of neo-classicism (and see John Wain, *C*,
pp. 28–31), was chiefly that the soldiers behaved in an
unsoldierly manner and that the play lacked a moral. Dr
Johnson, on the other hand, argued that '*Othello* has more

moral than almost any play' (*C*. p. 30), but moral – perhaps one should say, moralistic – critics have not been silenced by Johnson, much though they might not care to be associated too closely with Rymer. Rymer found the language of Othello and Iago hardly that 'of Souldiers and mighty Captains', 'the Murder shews nothing of a Souldier' (*C*, pp. 37, 38), which he called 'so unsouldierly an Execution' (p. 43). How ironical, then, looking at the play from Rymer's point of view, that Othello should describe himself to Lodovico as 'An honourable murderer, if you will' [v.ii.291]!

No one has been so extreme as Rymer in denying the play any claim to tragic status, but a number of critics have been uneasy about *Othello*. A. C. Bradley put well what may lie behind the minds of those who are critical of the play: 'even admitting that [*Othello*] is dramatically perhaps Shakespeare's greatest triumph, [some readers] still regard it with a certain distaste, or, at any rate, hardly allow it a place in their minds beside *Hamlet*, *King Lear* and *Macbeth*'. One reason for such a view, says Bradley (arguing against it), is that the play is concerned with sexual jealousy; another is that parts of the play appear 'shocking, even horrible'. The events dramatised are so brutal, so unnecessarily painful, that the play is 'rather sensational than tragic'. Yet, despite these charges of sensationalism, Bradley not only refutes them but sees the play as 'perhaps Shakespeare's greatest triumph'. The fact that the play has a long history of successful productions cannot be deployed to support Bradley here, because we might only be saying that what audiences most enjoy is sensationalism, not tragedy – and it isn't difficult to demonstrate that audiences have a fondness for the sensational.

Most critics are willing to grant that the play is a tragedy but they are at variance when trying to fathom out what kind of tragedy. Its ultimate horror to Harley Granville-Barker was that it was a tragedy 'without meaning'; to George Hibbard *Othello* 'is about the wanton destruction of happiness'; G. R. Elliott argued that it was a tragedy of pride, though the sub-title of his study of *Othello* and pride in the Renaissance, *Flaming Minister*, is 'A Study of *Othello* as Tragedy of Love and Hate'; a number of critics and scholars, Granville-Barker and S. L. Bethell among them, have described *Othello* as a domestic tragedy, a rare genre at that time; and Northrop Frye thought it 'a tragedy of isolation': 'The simplest and starkest account of the isolating of an unreflective temperament, however, is *Othello* . . . the one thing that isolates Othello [is] his black body', hence Brabantio's accusation of the '*unnatural* quality of Desdemona's love' for Othello (1957, p. 102; emphasis added).

The 'domestic' nature of *Othello* is intriguing and George Hibbard draws out coolly and dispassionately one important way in which *Othello* differs from Shakespeare's other tragedies: 'The unique quality of Shakespearian tragedy in general, distinguishing it from all other tragedy written at the time, is due in no small measure . . . to the fact that Shakespeare came to tragedy by way of the history play.' It was this that enabled Shakespeare to penetrate 'into the intimate connexions between the private decision and its public consequences, between the political action and its repercussions on the individual psyche' (*ShS 21*, p. 40). However, he argues, it is exactly this interconnexion that is *not* present in *Othello*, despite the play's opening with the alarums and excursions about a possible Turkish attack on Cyprus. So, it is not merely that *Othello* has, in the main, the domestic world as its milieu, but that another dimension, common to our experience of Shakespeare's tragedies, is present only at the start of the play, and is then dismissed: 'Othello's occupation' is quite clearly 'gone', as Hibbard points out. But what is even more worth noting is that Shakespeare does not merely dismiss the political world of Venice; he actually instigates it, as it were. In his source, Cinthio's story, there is no threat of imminent attack by the Turks; Othello goes to Cyprus 'in the regular course of duty as the replacement for a governor whose term of office has expired'. There is no question of Othello being chosen as 'the man for the crisis' in Cinthio: this is Shakespeare's invention, as is his dismissal of this strand of the story. Shakespeare is thus, quite deliberately, beginning in the historical–tragical genre and then moving away from that into a relatively novel domestic–tragic world. To us, with, say, the more recent inheritance of Ibsen and Strindberg to look back to, the domestic–tragic is a commonplace. Shakespeare was not only doing something relatively new but 'tricking the expectancy' of his audience by beginning in the genre they well knew – the quasi-political tragic world of *Hamlet*, *King Lear* and *Macbeth*.

Genre criticism, then, points to something highly individual about *Othello*. The domestic suggests an inwardness that the political milieu does not. This possibly supports the tragic isolation of which Northrop Frye speaks, although in the final outcome the tragic hero nearly always stands alone: think of Macbeth, for example, or, in our century, Arthur Miller's Willy Loman in *Death of a Salesman*. Hibbard speaks not of isolation but of contraction. Whereas Shakespeare's other tragedies expand outwards, he argues – in *Macbeth*, for instance, there is that seemingly curious excursion to the court of Edward the Confessor in London – *Othello* is a play of contraction:

> The action does not widen out, it narrows down as public business is increasingly excluded from it until it finds its catastrophe, not on the battle-field, nor in the presence of a court, but in a bedroom at night where two people, united by the closest of ties, speak at cross purposes and misunderstand each other disastrously . . . .   (*ShS 21*, p. 42)

What is destroyed is not 'a great potentiality for good' but, uniquely in Shakespeare, a relationship of rare beauty that has been 'realised and made concrete during the course of the play'.

Hibbard's approach (which I find convincing) can be supported by looking at the question of genre in another way. Over half a century ago, G. Wilson Knight said, '*Othello* is a story of intrigue rather than a visionary statement' (*C*, p. 72). Earlier Bradley, at the start of his first *Othello* lecture, had pointed out how much of the action and catastrophe of the play depended upon intrigue: 'Iago's intrigue occupies a position in the drama for which no parallel can be found in the other tragedies' – though he also stressed, 'We must not call the play a tragedy of intrigue as distinguished from a tragedy of character' (*C*, p. 179). Now, intrigue in drama is particularly associated with comedy. The poet W. H. Auden, writing chiefly about Iago, remarked, 'If *Othello* is a tragedy – and one certainly cannot call it a comedy – it is tragic in a peculiar way.' He went on to argue that Othello's fall was entirely the work of another – Iago – 'nothing he says or does originates with himself' (*C*, p. 199). Northrop Frye noted that Iago dominated the action of *Othello* 'almost to the point of being a tragic counterpart to the black king or evil magician of romance'. Such a 'comic vice' as Iago was 'something of an *architectus* or projection of the author's will' (1957, p. 216). (A suggestion that *Othello* is in some ways related to *commedia dell'arte* will be considered under 'Dramatic convention and decorum'.)

Of course (despite Rymer) the play is not comedy, but, Emrys Jones has pointed out how closely associated *Othello* is with comedic form. He notes particularly the parallels with *Much Ado about Nothing* – a play, like *Othello*, that has intrigue and amatory romance at its core, the rejection of a bride, features soldiers in peacetime engaged in wooing, and, perhaps most significantly, shows man as 'prey to illusion, unable to trust the evidence of his eyes (1971, pp. 121–2). Though as obviously a comedy as *Othello* is tragic, *Much Ado* comes close to tragedy and that moment is resolved by a sort of death–resurrection device (an artifice Shakespeare also uses in *The Winter's Tale* and, tragically, in *Romeo and Juliet*). And jealousy, so potent a tragic force in *Othello*, can be a subject of comedy, as in *The Merry Wives of Windsor*. Shakespeare also dramatised jealousy ambivalently in *The Winter's Tale*. Romance, a genre in which *The Winter's Tale* is often classified, is also significant in *Othello* and reference will be made to that in due course.

The question of *Othello* and its genre is not, therefore, quite so clear-cut as the simple title, *The Tragedy of Othello, the Moore of Venice*, would at first sight imply. Even to call it a domestic tragedy is, according to S. L. Bethell, to pay too little attention to its 'profoundly theological structure'. If Bethell is right, that offers another dimension in place of the political which Shakespeare dismisses. Again, that must be considered later.

Before turning to what might be termed a sub-genre within the play, it is worth noting Coleridge's *Table Talk* for 24 December 1822 as a rejoinder to those critics who see *Othello* as not only distinct from the three other 'great' tragedies, but in some way inferior:

> *Lear* is the most tremendous effort of Shakespeare as a poet; *Hamlet* as a philosopher or meditater; and *Othello* is the union of the two. There is something gigantic and unformed in the former two; but in the latter, everything assumes its due place and proportion and the whole mature powers of his mind are displayed in admirable equilibrium. (*ShS 21*, p. 10)

The sub-genre to which I referred affects Othello's final speech. This has been much castigated, notably by T. S. Eliot, who sees Othello as doing no more than 'cheering himself up'. He describes this as 'bovarysme', or 'the human will to see things as they are not' (*C*, pp. 70–1). Eliot's comment is taken up and pursued further by F. R. Leavis in 'Diabolic Intellect and the Noble Hero' (*C*, pp. 141–4). Othello, he claims, is 'self-dramatizing' and 'un-self-comprehending'; he is making a spectacle of himself. However, John Holloway argues that Eliot and Leavis seem unaware of the convention within which that speech was written and thus how Othello is to be interpreted: 'The last speech of a hero is no piece of private musing, but a conventional *genre*. It is the moment at which the character has a special privilege of comment: to sum up either his own life or what it stood for, or the causes of his death' (1961, p. 55). This convention, he shows, was widespread in Elizabethan drama and frequently used by Shakespeare. Here, not only is such an argument important to the critic; it must clearly be important for an actor, for there is a world of difference between playing a self-dramatising, un-self-comprehending character making a spectacle of himself as he attempts to cheer himself up, and playing one making a formal, conventional final statement, however passionately expressed.

Historical and social criticism

At first sight it seems a commonsensical approach to ask such questions as, 'What attitudes – what prejudices – did Shakespeare's first audiences bring to performances of *Othello*?', or, 'What were the implications of a black hero for Shakespeare and for the audiences who first came to see his play?', or, 'What "meaning" had this play for such an audience?'. Yes, the approach is commonsensical enough, but the problems are intractable. First, there was not 'one' Elizabethan audience: audiences varied then quite as much as they do now and, although a certain amount of information has been recovered about the kinds of people who went to the public theatres, there is much we don't know. Secondly, it is important to bear in mind that we cannot fully recover 'a meaning', 'a context' even for plays of our own day. There is a third important difficulty. The way we may respond emotionally to a character or situation today may conflict with how our knowledge of the past would tell us the author's contemporaries might be expected to respond. Thus, for *Othello*, public attitudes to a father's 'rights' over a daughter are very different now from what they were in Shakespeare's time. To an Elizabethan, as G. B. Harrison put it, 'For a young woman of Desdemona's social standing a runaway match even with a distinguished soldier was a gross breach of decency' (1951, p. 133). We may think Desdemona has been foolish, headstrong – or romantic. What Shakespeare thought we cannot guess, though he had two daughters, Susanna and Judith, and we sometimes gloss over the fact that in *Othello* Desdemona's marriage was mortal to her father, 'pure grief / Shore his old thread in twain' [v.ii.204–5]. If we can recapture only with difficulty Elizabethan attitudes in this respect, it is near impossible to have any feelings whatsoever about the threat to Cyprus. Emrys Jones puts the position succinctly (though for clarity in this extract from his account I have reversed the order of the sentences):

> The Turkish menace to Christendom was a fact of Shakespeare's entire lifetime; it remained of pressing concern to the West until late in the seventeenth century. Shakespeare could of course have taken for granted a general interest in the Ottoman empire which is very remote from what a modern audience brings to *Othello*.   (*ShS 21*, p. 51)

There are those who believe the aim of a modern reader should be to endeavour to respond to a work as would someone for whom that work was first intended; there are others who, recognising the difficulties attendant upon digging up the past, are content to study a work as if it were intended for an audience of our own time, ignoring that which is recondite and giving modern-day relevance to whatever it expresses. If the first approach present unsurmountable difficulties, the second may seriously distort the work and will deny us much of its richness. In Part Two of this little study a contextual compromise will be suggested, but first it is necessary to look at some of the ways critics and scholars have seen *Othello* in the context of Shakespeare's time. I have very briefly mentioned the historical context – the ever-present threat from the Ottoman empire – and will concentrate on three aspects: colour (to which most attention will be given), the Christian framework, and Shakespeare's source (which can be a critical approach in its own right).

Jane Adamson lists a number of aspects of *Othello* which, in her book-length study, she proposes not to discuss very fully and even ignore: double time; Iago's motives; *Othello* in the theatre; 'Christian elements' in the play – silence, she says, seems the best reply to those who claim they are important; and 'the importance of Othello's race'. In parenthesis she remarks, 'On the absurd debate about the exact shade of his skin I say nothing at all.' The significance of race in *Othello* she thinks 'has usually been over-emphasised by twentieth-century critics and producers, or given a wrong emphasis by being isolated from other elements in the drama'. The matter of Othello's colour (and his temperament and past history) are only significant in the play, she maintains, in so far as they represent 'given, indissoluble facts' as opposed to the 'more open and changeable areas' of characters' lives. What is dramatically significant is the way these may be confused by the characters and especially by Othello (Adamson, 1980, pp. 6–8). These limitations will be considered in Part Two, but here some account must be given of explorations of such aspects and of colour in particular.

Because we concentrate our attention on the work of Shakespeare, we sometimes imagine that Shakespeare's inclusion of black characters in his plays was exceptional in his time. Whereas Jews were few in number in England and rare in drama in Shakespeare's time, there were many blacks. Eldred Jones noted forty-three in masques, plays and pageants between 1510 and 1637, and several more appeared in Lord Mayors' pageants (listed by G. K. Hunter); Jones does not include Caliban. From *Tamburlaine* to *The Tempest* there were a score in addition to Shakespeare's four (two of whom, Aaron of *Titus Andronicus* and Morocco in *The Merchant of Venice*, were also Moors). In 1601, two or three years before *Othello* was first performed, Queen Elizabeth, 'discontented at the great number of "Negars and blackamoors" which are crept into the realm' arranged for Caspar Van Zeuden, a merchant of Lübeck, to transport them out of England (Eldred Jones, 1965, pp. 12–13). What was *different* about *Othello* as compared to any other play in which a black appeared, or as compared to Shakespeare's source – Cinthio – was the dramatic concentration given to the Moor as protagonist. In this sense, as G. K. Hunter explained, 'Shakespeare introduced a daring theatrical novelty – a black hero for a white community – a novelty which remains too daring for many recent theatrical audiences' (1967, p. 139).

Although Shakespeare's aim may have been no more than to heighten the contrast between 'given, indissoluble facts' and 'more open and changeable' characteristics, he could not possibly have been unaware of the attitudes to blacks in his own day, what blackness implied in religious terms, and even the animosity surrounding a particular Moor and his retinue resident in London about the time he was writing the play. He seems, also, to have touched on the fear aroused by the Ottoman empire in his selection of a name for his hero. In Cinthio, only the name 'Disdemona' is given; 'Othello', F. N. Lees proposed, seems to be suggested by Othoman (with a diminutive, *-ello*, added) after the founder of the Ottoman empire. That is Shakespeare's creation. Shakespeare was also working in a tradition which featured blackmen as 'bogey-man figures to clear the way before the main procession' (Hunter, 1967, p. 145), a tradition which equated 'black-faced men with wickedness' (p. 142), and which saw black as the badge of hell and sin. Traditionally, St George fought a black Moroccan in English folk-plays. Indeed, Bibles were still being printed in this century which had a black–red–white tricolour frontispiece marked sin–redemption–salvation. Hunter also points out that black was equated with sin and death not only in Europe but also in the ancient world and, ironically, in Africa. It is no chance that 'black' should be used frequently and significantly in the language of *Othello*. It is worth looking up such usages by Shakespeare as 'black-fac'd' for the evil Clifford in *Richard III*, I.*ii*. 158; 'black-fac'd night' – desire's foul nurse – in *Venus and Adonis*, l. 773; and in *The Rape of Lucrece*, 'black-fac'd cloud' at l. 547 and especially 'black-fac'd storms' at l. 1518. What 'black' evoked in poetic and religious terms was very strong in Shakespeare's time and undoubtedly informed racial attitudes. It is inconceivable that Shakespeare was not harnessing innate prejudice to his dramatic ends, even though those ends may be discussed simply in Dr Adamson's terms. Prejudice is deep-seated and continuous, perhaps nowhere more incongruously illustrated than in the oft-repeated explanation of a Victorian lady from Maryland who maintained that, 'in studying the play of *Othello*, I have always *imagined* its hero a white man' (Hunter, 1967, p. 140, quoting the Variorum *Othello*).

Whether Othello is to be seen as black or as tawny has been frequently discussed and frequently dismissed as irrelevant. To G. K. Hunter, such arguments are worthy of study only 'as documents of prejudice' (p. 139). But there is a genuine discrepancy, and not only is avoiding it a kind of inverted prejudice: we might miss a dramatic point. Othello is called a Moor – in the play's sub-title, in the play itself, and in Cinthio. Further, on 8 August 1600 there landed at Dover a Moorish embassy to the court of Queen Elizabeth. They aroused interest, naturally, but by the time they left in February 1601 they had become much disliked. It so happens we know precisely what the ambassador, Abd el-Ouahed ben Messaoud ben Mohammed Anoun, looked like, for he had his portrait painted. This survives – it hangs in the Shakespeare Institute, University of Birmingham – and is reproduced in *Shakespeare Survey 11* (1958). The Moorish ambassador was clearly tawny, as Coleridge among others (including Bradley) believed Othello to be: 'Mr C. ridiculed the idea of making Othello a negro. He was a gallant Moor, of royal blood, combining a high sense of Spanish and Italian feeling' (*C*, p. 54). Yet at iii.iii.263 Othello plainly states, 'Haply for I am black', and it is as black that he has in recent times been presented. The argument is not pointless, nor a mark of our own prejudice, if it makes us realise not only that Shakespeare's Moor is black, so encapsulating a whole range of latent feelings in his audiences then and now, but of a particular blackness. This has been put well by Richard David: 'we must avoid the negations of Shakespeare's intentions implied, on the one hand, by making Othello no alien but an elegantly sun-tanned European, and on the other by Olivier's representation of him as a "modern" negro, out of Harlem rather than Barbary', and, he goes on, 'rather devil-worshipper than devil' (1976, p. 46), which conveniently takes us to another aspect of historical and social interpretation.

Despite any lingering doubts there might be about the

precise shade of Othello's complexion, there can be none that
'A black/white opposition is clearly built into the play at
every level: factually, physically, visually, poetically,
psychologically, symbolically, morally and religiously'
(Sanders, 1984, p. 14). Although, as has been noted, there are
those who would dismiss 'Christian elements' in the play, they
may be on sure ground only when they rebuke those who insist
upon the 'central importance' of a Christian interpretation.
Given the imagery of the play and the common ground of a
Christian framework to Elizabethan life (however differently
that might be understood, and however much under attack), it
is hardly surprising if some critics have been able to find a
Christian dimension to *Othello*. Parallels such as those pointed
out by Roy W. Battenhouse (for instance, between Othello's
'Put up your bright swords' and Christ's injunction to Peter
at Gethsemane, 'Put up your sword into the sheath', or
between Othello's 'I kissed thee ere I killed thee' and the kiss of
Judas) may not convince everyone, though it is hard to argue
away the number and placements of diabolic imagery in the
play as set out by S. L. Bethell (see next section). At the very
least, Othello's suicide begs to be interpreted within the
Christian framework, and it is hard not to see an inversion of
God's declaration 'I am that I am' (Exodus 3:14) in Iago's 'I
am not what I am' [I.i.65] – the devil as opposite of the divine
(*ShS 21*, p. 73). What these diabolic images do, argues Bethell,
is 'serve the true purpose of poetic drama, to show the
underside, as it were, of ordinary life' (p. 79).

Related to religious interpretations are those which have
sought to show how, to an Elizabethan, references to witchcraft
may be more telling than they are to us. David Kuala, for
example, has pointed out that Shakespeare wrote the play
when public anxiety in England over the dangers of witchcraft
was intense (1966). Shakespeare uses the word 'witchcraft'
eighteen times in his works, four of them in *Othello*. To us,
accusations that Othello bewitched Desdemona – used drugs,
charms, conjurations, mighty magic [I.iii.91–2] – seem more
poetic than actual. When Brabantio cannot believe his
daughter has been won without witchcraft [I.iii.64], and
Othello claims that the only witchcraft he has used is telling the
story of his life, we miss the full implication this had for an
Elizabethan.

Most editions of *Othello* will give extracts at least of Cinthio's story, which was the principal though not sole source of Shakespeare's play, and will almost certainly retain the changes Shakespeare made. Source criticism is important not for the mere listing of differences but because changes may well show us how the dramatist 'saw' his work and enable us to guess more accurately what effects he wished to achieve. Some changes were essential: characters had to have names – but the choice of names could be significant, as suggested above for Othello's name. On the other hand, Shakespeare was sometimes careless with names, so that more than one character may appear in a play with the same name. In even such relatively simple matters, critical tact is essential.

As comparisons with Cinthio are so readily available, it is only necessary here to gesture in this direction and to draw out one or two points. First, it has been suggested that Cinthio was more remote to an Elizabethan audience than in fact he was. It is true that most of the audience would not have known the original story, but a dramatist – like a common-or-garden lecturer – has to be on his guard against even those few of his audience who are well informed. To an artist such as Shakespeare it was always worthwhile providing some additional spice 'for those who knew', for the initiates. Secondly, although we know of no English translation of Cinthio's *Hecatommithi*, that does not mean one didn't exist, but, in any case, in 1584 a French translation was published which would have made the stories more widely known even if until then they had then been available only in their original Italian. (Arguments as to whether Shakespeare used Cinthio's original Italian or Chappuys's French version, or both, are well summarised in Norman Sanders's edition.) One relatively minor change which Shakespeare made is worth bringing out, particularly as it affects historical criticism. Shakespeare thought it worthwhile to modernise the events slightly. Cinthio purported to tell true stories. The events he recounts are supposed to have taken place in 1544 and are not related to any specific threat by the Turks; Shakespeare links his story to events which took place in 1570 (see G. M. Matthews, '*Othello* and the Dignity of Man'). In addition to providing an initial political dimension, this gives the story a kind of immediacy, a pointedness it might otherwise not have had. It becomes a little closer to 'actual experience'.

However, as Norman Sanders summarises his list of changes, 'No such cataloguing of specific plot and character changes can convey the way in which the sordid story of Italian intrigues became the greatest domestic tragedy in the English language' (1984, p. 9). Such is the measure of the difference between a competent storyteller and a genius.

Dramatic convention and decorum

Because so much study of Shakespeare – and, indeed, of all dramatists – is done from the printed text, mainly, sometimes entirely, divorced from the play in performance, a distorted, partial view of a dramatic work becomes only too common. This applies as much to critics as to students. The inverse can also, unfortunately, occur: theatre people may ignore or even be contemptuous of scholarship and criticism. It ought to be obvious that the most intelligent and satisfying understanding of a drama will marry scholarship and dramatic practice. Even as formidable a critic as A. C. Bradley had, as Helen Gardner put it, 'a defective feeling for the stage. He took insufficient account of the distinction between characterization in a novel and characterization in a play.' The former creates characters who 'come to life in our imagination'; the latter, those 'an actor is to bring to life on the stage' (ShS 21, p. 81). It is nowadays much more common to appeal to theatrical experience. This can take two forms: reference to what has happened in performances over the years, and research into dramatic conventions. A crude but obvious example of the latter is the convention that we accept that the heroine of an opera is dying of tuberculosis even though she expresses her anguish in singing a demanding aria. Where one often finds convention overlooked is in the assumption that a character in a poetic drama who has lengthy and elaborate speeches must himself be a poet – Richard II is quite frequently described as failing as a king because he is a poet manqué. The convention of the soliloquy also can cause misunderstanding. Levin Schücking and Edgar Elmer Stoll early pointed to the deficiencies of a study-bound approach to drama. Stoll (who published important essays on *Othello* in 1915 and on *Hamlet* four years later), explained in *Art and Artifice in Shakespeare,*

> The trouble with Shakespeare criticism . . . is that it has been prompted and guided by the spirit of literalism. The play has been thought to be a psychological document, not primarily a play, a structure, both interdependent and independent, the parts mutually, and sufficiently, supporting and explaining each other; and the characters have been taken for the separable copies of reality. At bottom the mistake is the same as that of the actors, who, as Heine said, were in his day concerned only for the characterisation, 'not at all for the poetry, and still less for the art'.   (1933, pp. 48–9)

Stoll was particularly telling in his argument that, in believing Iago's slanders, Othello was deceived, not because those slanders were convincing *per se*, nor because of character-psychology, but because of the convention of 'the calumniator credited'. This was a *donné*, a given, stock circumstance, a starting-point for what ensued. If this is correct, it undercuts demands for psychological motivation. He explained, 'Though less obvious and external, it is an artifice of constructive character, like other traditional forms of deception in fiction, such as disguise and eavesdropping' (p. 6). He showed how commonly this convention was used by Shakespeare. A good example of the convention of the slanderer believed, combined with disguise and complicated eavesdropping, leading to near-tragic results, can be seen in *Much Ado about Nothing*. Of course, that play is a comedy and we seem able to accept such conventions more readily in comedy than in tragedy, especially when blatantly used. But the convention, Stoll argues, is applicable to *Othello*. (Its use supports the argument that this tragedy has a comedic structure – see 'Genre criticism', above.) Stoll admits that this conventional 'intrusion of the villain' is 'a mechanical device', but he points out that 'there is something mechanical in most art' and he instances the fugue and the symphony. What matters is how the convention is used (p. 20).

F. R. Leavis, girding at Bradley's interpretation of Iago, even at Iago's getting to himself one of Bradley's two lectures devoted to *Othello*, whereas Othello shares the other with

Desdemona, protests vigorously at the very idea of Iago's supposed devilish 'intellectual superiority' and maintains that he is 'subordinate and merely ancillary'. He goes on, 'He is not much more than a necessary piece of dramatic mechanism – that at any rate is a fit reply to the view of Othello as necessary material and provocation for a display of Iago's fiendish intellectual superiority' (*C*, p. 125). But this, as Kenneth Muir has more elegantly suggested, is throwing the baby out with the bath-water. Leavis was right to react against those 'who exaggerate [Iago's] intellectual superiority', but such emphasis, in Muir's words, 'immeasurably impoverishes the metaphysical content of the play' (1972, p. 105). By the way he uses the words 'devilish' and 'fiendish' one gets the impression that Leavis is denying that characteristic of Iago. One has the stage device ('dramatic mechanism') without the dramatic inheritance. Stoll's argument for Iago's dramatic conventional nature might not carry conviction at all points – or rather seem a total account of Iago – but it really is difficult to imagine an Elizabethan audience not consciously or subconsciously relating the character of Iago to the still-current dramatic tradition. Leavis wishes to insist that *Othello* is poetic drama, 'a dramatic poem and not a psychological novel written in dramatic form and draped in poetry' (*C*, p. 123). But concern to dismiss Bradley (who at times seems more a subject of attack than *Othello* is the subject of interpretation and evaluation) and to concentrate on the poetry to the exclusion of other aspects ensures a lack of balance and a thinness in response. Given the concern with the poetry of the play, it is a trifle ironic that more weight is not given to the diabolic aspects of the play, and of Iago in particular, which stem from the poetry. This characteristic has been finely analysed by S. L. Bethell. As Muir summarises it, 'It is difficult not to accept [his] view that Shakespeare introduced sixty-four "diabolic" images into the play to show "Othello and Iago as exemplifying and participating in the age-long warfare of Good and Evil"' (Muir, 1972, p. 105; Bethell, *ShS 21*, p. 71). In effect, Bethell's analysis of the poetic imagery marches well with Stoll's Iago as a product of a dramatic tradition. And, picking up Stoll again, what matters is *how* the creative artist uses his devices. The pattern of usage of these images cannot but be significant. There are more such images than in any other play by

Shakespeare. Next in order is (the shorter) *Macbeth* with thirty-seven. But what is most interesting is the way it is Iago who begins using such images, Othello who takes them over as the play progresses, and that Desdemona has none – 'the more angel she' [v.ii.130] – thus:

Act	I	II	III	IV	V
Iago	8	6	3	1	0
Othello	0	1	9	10	6

Further, no such images occur in Cinthio, Shakespeare's main source. To Bethell, this has the effect of developing poetically 'an important underlying theme' of the play (*ShS 21*, pp. 68–71). This is not a view universally shared: Helen Gardner, for example, argues that the very frequency of such images 'deprives them of any imaginative potency', thus ' "Devil" is a cliché in this play, a tired metaphor for "very bad", as "angel" is for "very good" ' (*C*, pp. 149, 150).

Leah Scragg, in a valuable essay, 'Iago – Vice or Devil?', re-examined the arguments for Iago's heritage. She briefly rehearses the case made by Brandl, Cushman and especially Bernard Spivack (in *Shakespeare and the Allegory of Evil*) which seeks to show how Iago shares characteristics associated with the comic Vice of the morality plays. Dr Scragg, however, argues that Iago is to be related more directly to the Devil of earlier drama than to the Vice – though, as she points out, they can share attributes. Thus the Devil in *Mind, Will and Understanding*, a morality play of the latter part of the fifteenth century, in 'Vice-like manner' boasts of his cunning 'and then proceeds to share with the audience his intention to corrupt Mind, Will and Understanding, thus bringing the soul to damnation' (*ShS 21*, p. 58). The Devil in this play also puts on a pose 'as the friend of the victim', a disguise originating in the serpent of Genesis. As she points out, she is not the first to associate Iago with the devil as agent of hell or as play-character. Stoll had 'pointed to the ambiguity of (Iago's) motivation', which partook of 'the nature of the Devil' as a character in the earlier drama; she quotes Coleridge's description of Iago as 'a being next to the devil, and only not quite devil' (p. 61); Bradley remarked that 'to compare Iago with the Satan of *Paradise Lost* seems almost absurd, so immensely does Shakespeare's man *exceed* Milton's Fiend in evil' (1904, p. 207). The stress on 'exceed' in that quotation is mine; but note how Bradley sees Iago – not as a character but as a man, as if Iago were a real person. After reviewing a number of critics' descriptions of Iago, Dr Scragg concludes with Dr Leavis's 'famous pronouncement' that Iago is no more than 'a necessary piece of dramatic mechanism' and the repudiation of Iago's fiendishness and an assertion of his humanity by Marvin Rosenberg (1961, pp. 170–1).

Without being in any way dogmatic, Dr Scragg argues – convincingly, I think – that Iago derives 'from the Devil rather than the Vice' of earlier drama, but 'it would be overstating the position to assert categorically that Iago's characterization is *necessarily* derived from a traditional stage presentation of the Devil' (*ShS 21*, p. 64). If this association with the stage Devil is accepted (with the implications it conveys of the devil of the spirit world), then the ultimate motive for Iago's hatred of Othello, Desdemona and Cassio 'is his denial of the values they affirm': 'It is the hatred of Satan for the sanctity of Adam and Eve, the hatred of a being who is forced to recognize a virtue he cannot share and constantly desires. Hence the "daily beauty" of the lives of Othello, Cassio, and Desdemona is a constant affront to him.' But, if this identification is accepted, there is a further implication which has profound implications for our understanding of the play's conclusion. In the following quotation, the emphasis is mine:

> At the close of the play, when [Iago] has corrupted Othello's mind, destroyed both him and Desdemona, when, for them, *Paradise has been lost*, Iago is dragged away to the tortures that are his element. He does not die at the end of the play, he is not to be put rapidly to death. He is to linger in pain like the powers of whom he is the instrument. Iago follows the pattern laid down in the garden of Eden and repeated over and over again in Christian literature by the archetypal adversary of mankind. (p. 64)

In this approach, Iago betakes of stage Devil as representative of devil-as-archetypal-adversary of mankind and it implies an end for Othello very different from that envisaged by Horatio for Hamlet in his 'flights of angels sing thee to thy rest' after

Hamlet's death. It is an approach, too, in direct opposition to
Bradley's. He rejected the idea that Iago was a 'being who
hates good simply because it is good, and loves evil purely for
itself'. This, 'if not a psychological impossibility' would ensure
Iago is 'not a *human* being' (1904, p. 209; the emphasis is
Bradley's). It also offers a far richer dimension to Iago that Dr
Leavis's dramatic mechanism. It does not deny Iago human
credibility, of course, though that does not make the character
'human'. The devil assumes the cloak of humankind to suit his
purposes, at least in dramatic literature. Finally, drawing on
Marvin Rosenberg's work on the stage history of *Othello*, Dr
Scragg reports his findings that 'Iago's role is unsatisfying
when played as Vice rather than Devil' (*ShS 21*, p. 65 n. 31).

Dramatic conventions have been noted elsewhere in *Othello*,
though they are of rather lesser significance, Jealousy (which
is, in any case, a fact of life) can in drama be aroused on the
slightest grounds – as if were a *donné* – and Othello has also been
seen as an example of the braggart soldier of classical drama, an
interpretation regarded by Professor Muir as 'surely mistaken'
(1978, p. 102). Could Othello really be a tragic version of
Pistol? Could they both spring from the same dramatic stock?
Hardly. This is very well demonstrated by another study of
Othello and the dramatic tradition: Barbara Mendonça's
'*Othello*: A Tragedy Built on a Comic Structure' (*ShS 21*, 31–8),
that structure being *commedia dell'arte*. Structure, character and
conflict are examined. Iago is related to the *zanni*, the
confidence-trickster, especially such as Brighella, the servant
who seeks his own advancement rather than his master's;
Brabantio is related to Pantalone; Desdemona is an *amorosa* or
innamorata, and Emilia a *servetta*. However, Barbara Mendonça
goes on to say that 'It would be pointless to look for further
parallels in minor characters. . . . Even more pointless would
be to include any possibility of an interpretation of Othello into
this scheme.' She reasons that 'the very essence of the conflict
lies in the fact he is not a super-subtle Venetian'. This
conflict arises from different moral convictions: those of Othello
'are more impassioned and more exacting than those of the
super-subtle Venetians who lived in a world of excessive
civilization whose social usages . . . had . . . become empty of
significance' (p. 36). She concludes that 'the progressive
shifting from the Venetian values of *commedia dell'arte* to

Othello's extreme, rough and violent ones must be the key to
the appalling emergence of a tragedy from what should be,
from the initial given dramatic values, a comic situation'
(p. 37) – which takes us back to genre criticism.

Convention can be seen in another guise – as decorum.
T. McAlindon has attempted to show how Shakespeare's
'understanding and representation of human behaviour – of
words and deeds – was affected by this comprehensive doctrine
of decorum' (1973, p. 3). *Othello* is interpreted from this point of
view as 'the tragedy of the tongue and its terrible potency'
(p. 18); 'the cause of disorder can be traced to the abuse of the
play's two fundamental norms, timeliness and truth'. In
Othello, decorum is broken by a marriage in secret without
consent and its tardy consummation; the bridal-chamber
becomes first brothel and then the setting for murder (p. 93).
This, rather than an explication, suggests an added dimension
to the play, but it is of help in assessing the nature of the
soliloquies.

The soliloquy is a particularly important convention in
Elizabethan drama. Professor Wolfgang Clemen has indicated
ways in which Shakespeare exploited the possibilities offered
by this conventional device. He 'constantly discovers new
possibilities inherent in the soliloquy' (1964, p. 6). Bernard
Spivak has shown how the soliloquy may be used to convey
necessary information (1958). Professor Nevill Coghill finds
this too limiting of *Othello*. It is significant that, whereas Othello
has three soliloquies, Iago has eight. Iago's soliloquies do far
more than provide necessary information. They contrast with
those of another villain, Richard III, in that Richard's 'win his
hearers over to him' whereas Iago's first three soliloquies 'are
graded in order of heinousness, the foulest last . . . to create hatred
for him' in the audience. They also 'provide a living image of a
man who is the opposite of what he appears to be', of 'I am not
what I am' [I.i.66]. Whereas the first three soliloquies offer a
'progressive clarification' of Iago's schemes, 'they also offer a
progressive exhibition of the evil in him'. The five that follow
give 'practical shape to his thoughts, rather than a
psychological' (*C*, pp. 227–32).

It is important in the light of such explanations of the use of
the soliloquy not to assume that that which is rooted in
convention is unchanging. Convention can provide a short cut

to understanding for the audience – something vital to a dramatist whose time for telling his story is brief, at least as compared to that of a nineteenth-century novelist – but, as with every other aspect of his art, the great creative talent moulds and modifies the conventional. But dramatic (and social) convention means that, if a play is 'read' simply as a poem on a page, interpretations can be over-simplified if not falsified.

Character and psychological criticism

No critical approach has led to more disagreement and aroused more animosity than has the analysis of the character of Othello and, to a lesser degree, Iago. The language of some critics in attacking those whose views they do not share has been at times personal and vituperative – no advertisement for a humane discipline. For some students this can distract the reader from matters of moment that such a critic might also be raising. Although such antagonisms are not peculiar to the study of *Othello*, that play seems to have attracted a disproportionate share of such abuse. It might be of interest to try to tease out in a general study of twentieth-century criticism what it is in this play that strikes such chilling responses by one critic to another.

Writing character-sketches of participants in a drama is a long-established custom. Thus, Shakespeare's contemporary Ben Jonson provided pen-portraits of the characters of *Every Man out of his Humour* for the edition of 1616. Asper is described as 'an ingenious and free spirit, eager, and constant in reproof, without fear controlling the world's abuses. One, whom no servile hope of gain, or frosty apprehension of danger, can make to be a parasite, either to time, place, or opinion'. From the early twentieth century, school texts of Shakespeare's plays frequently included descriptions of 'the characters', but the approach shifted into a different gear when, in 1910, Ernest Jones, a psychoanalyst who studied under Freud, published his first psychoanalytic interpretation of Hamlet. (His most famous study, *Hamlet and Oedipus*, appeared in 1949.) Psychological and analytical studies can be revealing – those of Prince Hal and Falstaff do throw new light on these characters and their relationship.

It is important to realise that for artistic reasons many characters in drama may *not* be intended to be life portraits. Jonson in particular worked within an aesthetic that did not require 'rounded' characters, and it is a mistake of the first order to assess his characters as if they were intended to be other than they are. However, if a dramatist intends characters to be 'life-like', it is hardly surprising such characters may have traits in common with real-life people. It is a short step to applying psychological and psychoanalytical analysis to characters as if they were actual people of the living world, and then another short, and very dangerous step, to imagining play-characters as if they were real people, creating for them aspects of their 'lives' to round out their characters even more. Further, it is arguable that the artist controls, to a greater or lesser extent, his creations (even though some contemporary writers like to promulgate a fiction that their characters determine their own fates), whereas professional analysis of the individual should take into account the whole person and that will include his or her dream-world.

We are here concerned with character analysis, but it ought to be mentioned that the psychological approach can be applied to the creative artist, seeking out what it is that makes a creative writer the artist he is. Wilbur Scott gives as an example Edmund Wilson's essays in *The Wound and the Bow* (1972, p. 72). In that collection there is a study of Dickens and a passing reference to Shakespeare hints at how the approach is applied. Wilson is speaking of artists caught between two social classes (like Dickens), or between two civilisations (like Henry James). This, he suggests, enables the writer 'to dramatize contrasts and study interrelations which the dweller in one world cannot know'. He goes on, 'Perhaps something of the sort was true even of Shakespeare, between the provincial bourgeoisie and the Court'; a writer's 'dramatic scope' may at least partly result from 'a social maladjustment'. This could be particularly relevant for *Othello* given what was said at the end of the preceding section about Othello being caught between two cultures. There is also, in this application of psychoanalysis to the author, a hint that Jonson anticipated such contemporary critical approaches in his drama. His character Asper is matched in *Every Man out of his Humour* by Macilente: both represent Jonson himself, and, as the description Jonson added shows, Macilente presents him 'out of his humour' because 'wanting that place in the world's account which he thinks his merit capable of'. Though it is dismissed as an 'irrelevance' by Helen Gardner when disposing of Maud Bodkin's treatment of *Othello* (*C*, p. 167 n. 5), psychological criticism, used as sharply as by Jonson and with discretion, is valuable and has the best of artistic pedigrees.

It is not difficult to understand why Shakespeare's major characters have been subjected to psychological analysis as if they were living human beings. They are fictions – but they are incredibly life like, even larger than life. The great German critic Schlegel, writing nearly two hundred years ago, hit the nail on the head:

> He gives us the history of minds. . . . Of all poets, perhaps, he alone has portrayed the mental diseases, melancholy, delirium, lunacy, with such inexpressible and . . . definite truth, that the physician may enrich his observations from them in the same manner as from real cases. (1840, II, 136–7)

This, half a century before Freud was born! In an interesting Appendix to her *Archetypal Patterns in Poetry*, Maud Bodkin discusses 'Psychological Criticism and Dramatic Conventions'. In this she defends herself for writing of Othello in the main body of the book as if he were an actual man. This, she says, is simply for 'conciseness of expression'. Nothing, perhaps, illustrates more clearly and more honestly the difficulty of avoiding thinking of Shakespeare's major characters as if they were living persons. But the temptation must be resisted.

Inevitably psychological studies of Othello and Iago have often centred on the *psychological relationship* of the two characters. Occasionally critics have gone so far as to see Iago as 'the shadow-side of Othello' (Bodkin, 1934, p. 245). Some superficial support for Iago as the 'projected image of the submerged fears, hidden deep within Othello' has been given in the theatre, where over the past hundred years there have been productions in which the actors playing Othello and Iago have exchanged roles in alternating performances. A neat and convincing relationship is given by G. K. Hunter:

The relationship between these two is developed in terms of appearance and reality. Othello controls the reality of action; Iago the 'appearance' of talk about action; Iago the Italian is isolated (even from his wife), envious, enigmatic (even to himself), self-centered; Othello the 'extravagant and wheeling stranger' is surrounded and protected by a network of duties, obligations, esteems, pious to his father-in-law, deferential to his superiors, kind to his subordinates, loving to his wife. To sum up, assuming that *soul* is reality and *body* is appearance, we may say that Iago is the white man with the black soul while Othello is the black man with the white soul.   (1967, p. 151)

Although not the first to think of play characters in real-life terms, it is A. C. Bradley who stands out as the critic with whom this tendency is most associated. The reason is simple: his analyses of characters in *Shakespearean Tragedy*, and his comprehension of the philosophy of Shakespeare's tragedy, were so masterful, so compelling and so engagingly expressed that his book dominated criticism for several decades. It is a measure of its lasting value that, despite the opposition of such scholars as Stoll and Schücking, and the swingeing assault of F. R. Leavis, his stock still rides high – and with justice. It is not difficult to discount in one's reading the slippage into assumptions about the real-life nature of his subjects, and, even if one disagrees with his arguments, his passionate engagement with his subject is perennially attractive. J. I. M. Stewart put it very simply, referring to Bradley's 'genius' as 'the writer of the best book on Shakespeare' (1963, p. 292). (Four pages later he describes Harley Granville-Barker as offering character-studies in his *Prefaces* 'almost in direct line of Bradley', only informed by a closer knowledge of the stage.)

The two principal views of Othello are well described by Norman Sanders in his New Cambridge edition of the play as being based

as much on the ideals of the critics themselves as on their reading of the play. Johnson's picture of the Moor is clearly that of the sedentary intellectual who elsewhere said, 'Every man thinks meanly of himself for not having been a soldier, or not having been at sea'. Similarly, the version of Leavis and Eliot is that of all people for whom introspection, self-awareness, deliberate thought, balanced judgement and the contented inhabitation of a dilemma are more congenial than a life of action and passionate involvement. As the play in the theatre draws the audience emotionally into its world, so the play in the study challenges the reader's own intellectual convictions and assumptions.   (1984, p. 24)

To Bradley, Othello was the most romantic of Shakespeare's heroes: 'He does not belong to our world, and he seems to enter it we know not whence – almost as if from wonderland. There is something mysterious in his descent from men of royal siege; in his wanderings in vast deserts and among marvellous peoples . . . .' To Bradley, Othello is the greatest poet of all Shakespeare's heroes (*C*, p. 57). But, 'Othello's mind, for all its poetry, is very simple. He is not observant. . . . He is quite free from introspection, and is not given to reflection . . . [with] Hamlet . . . he shares a great openness and trustfulness of nature . . . he has little experience of the corrupt products of civilised life, and is ignorant of European women.' Though Bradley considers that Othello has greater dignity than any other of Shakespeare's men, and a massive calm, 'he is by nature full of the most vehement passion' (p. 59). Then, in a famous passage, 'His trust, where he trusts, is absolute. Hesitation is almost impossible to him' (p. 60). Bradley takes up those critics who consider Othello jealous by nature by denying even that he was easily jealous. Such critics 'seem to think that it was inexcusable in him to feel any suspicion of his wife at all; and they blame him for never suspecting Iago'; but Othello was 'thorough in his trust', he was newly married, and he was 'totally ignorant of the thoughts and the customary morality of Venetian women' (pp. 61–3), by which he seems to imply 'immorality'.

Bradley analyses Iago with even greater thoroughness (a seeming imbalance that has disturbed some critics, though it is quite likely that more attention will be paid to Falstaff than Hal; critical puzzles are not necessarily directly proportional to hierarchical standing). Bradley remarks on Iago's 'very remarkable powers both of intellect and will', his (limited) insight into human nature, his ingenuity, quickness, versatility; 'Not Socrates himself, not the ideal sage of the Stoics, was more lord of himself than Iago appears to be' (1904, p. 218). His creed 'is that absolute egoism is the only rational and proper attitude, and that conscience or honour or any kind of regard for others is an absurdity' (p. 219). Bradley then turns to what motivates Iago – a puzzle to so many people. He dismisses critical 'motive-hunting' by explaining that it is Iago who is motive-hunting; he is 'pondering his design, and unconsciously trying to justify it to himself' (p. 226). This is ingenious but has not convinced everyone. But he does give, if not motives, explanations for his character. Iago, thinks Bradley, 'is keenly sensitive to anything that touches his pride or self-esteem' (p. 221); 'The most delightful thing to such a man would be something that gave an extreme satisfaction to his sense of power and superiority . . . the triumphant exertion of his abilities . . . the excitement of danger' (p. 228); 'longing to satisfy the sense of power is . . . the strongest of the forces that drives him on'; he is 'not simply a man of action; he is an artist' (p. 230); finally, he is destroyed 'by the power that he attacked, the power of love' (p. 236). As will be appreciated from the range of page references, this is but a bare skeleton of Bradley's analysis, but it will suffice, perhaps, to indicate his approach, and a powerfully romantic approach it is. But there *is* an imbalance in Bradley, though it has nothing to do with the *amount* of attention given to Othello and Iago. It can be summed up in his words, 'we are now in a position to consider the rise of Iago's tragedy' (p. 222). This *must* be a misconception and it must be taken into account when reading Bradley.

F. R. Leavis's 'Diabolic Intellect and the Noble Hero' provides an important readjustment of Bradley's account. It is, for many readers, marred by its personal attacks on Bradley. Bradley is rebuked for failing to make his approach 'consistently and with moderate intelligence'; Leavis writes of Bradley's 'misdirected scrupulosity' and 'comical solemnity', judges his argument 'grossly and palpably false to the evidence it offers to weigh', and complains that, alas, Bradley 'is still a very potent and mischievous influence' (*C*, pp. 23–5). Now the balance has tilted in the other direction. Thus, John Bayley argues that the ' "heroic mode" *is* the love mode, as Dr Leavis must surely have seen if he were not so determined that love in the play is a negative and hollow thing, existing only to be shown up' (*C*, p. 179); a long appendix to John Holloway's *The*

Story of the Night shows in detail the hollowness of much of Dr Leavis's case and concludes, 'What Dr Leavis takes as the decisive proof of how Othello's love is at bottom voluptuous sensuality is no proof at all' (1961, p. 164); and Norman Sanders counterbalances Leavis's view of Bradley's influence being still potent by suggesting that it is Leavis's essay that 'has had far too much influence . . . despite the fact that his remarkable gifts are clearly of the type that make him about as naturally incapable of appreciating drama as it is possible to be' (1984, p. 23). But Dr Leavis should not be dismissed any more than Bradley: both should be read, but warily. Whereas (in Leavis's view) Othello and Desdemona were presented by Bradley as near-faultless, Othello's very virtues being turned against him, his downfall caused by external evil, Leavis finds Othello hollow. Othello's character is dominated by his capacity for self-dramatisation, self-idealisation becomes blindness, his nobility 'an obtuse and brutal egotism' and self-pride stupidity; 'Othello's noble lack of self-knowledge is shown as humiliating and disastrous' (*C*, p. 135). Iago, to whom Bradley devoted so much attention, is reduced to 'a necessary piece of dramatic mechanism' and his role is 'subordinate and merely ancillary'. Leavis's arguments are convincing enough as one reads, but they fail to take into account the experience of the play as performed. It may be that Leavis epitomises an intellectual approach (and misapprehension) of an emotional conflict whereas Bradley is responding to the emotions. Where Leavis surely is right is in asserting that Bradley is incorrect in saying 'Iago's plot is Iago's character in action' (p. 124) – or, as Bradley writes, even less defensibly, 'the rise of Iago's tragedy'. Yet, W. H. Auden can begin by saying that for this tragedy we 'must be primarily occupied, not with its official hero but with its villain'; further, he maintains, 'I cannot think of any other play in which only one character performs personal actions – all the *deeds* are Iago's – and all the others without exception only exhibit behaviour' (*C*, p. 199).

The differences in approach to Othello are well summed up by the contrasting attitudes in Othello's final speech. To T. S. Eliot, Othello is simply cheering himself up:

He is endeavouring to escape reality, he has ceased to think about Desdemona, and is thinking about himself. Humility is the most difficult of all virtues to achieve; nothing dies harder than the desire to think well of oneself. Othello succeeds in turning himself into a pathetic figure, by adopting an *aesthetic* rather than a moral attitude, dramatising himself against his environment. He takes in the spectator, but the human motive is primarily to take in himself. I do not believe that any writer has ever exposed this *bovarysme*, the human will to see things as they are not, more clearly than Shakespeare.   (*C*, pp. 70–1)

Leavis agreed, finding in Othello a tendancy to sentimentalise and finding his 'self-dramatization as un-selfcomprehending as before' (*C*, p. 141). D. A. Traversi also follows Eliot, regarding the speech as 'the dupe's attempt at self-justification in an irrelevant pose . . . a splendid declamation, but it is also largely beside the point'. He is 'unable to cope with the complicated business of living' (1956, pp. 148–9). It is hard to imagine how a character so denigrated could be the hero of one of the world's greatest and most moving tragedies! Mention has already been made in the previous section that this speech is 'no piece of private musing, but a conventional *genre*, to be understood within the decorum of "a final summation" by stage characters of their role' (Holloway, 1966, p. 55). To John Bayley, Othello is convincing us that 'he means what he says, and that he is sure his suicide will cut him off from the last hope of mercy' (*C*, p. 197). Such an act is thus one that takes great courage and arises from a character psychologically poles apart from that envisaged by Eliot, Leavis and Traversi. For Holloway, Othello's character is also far removed from that as assessed by this trio. Othello's act is 'no mere self-indulgent re-enactment' when 'he took vengeance on a little enemy of his society'. He has come to realise that 'The justice he wrought upon Desdemona was a false justice. This is not. The pattern of the tragedy is complete at last' (1961, p. 56). A subtle analysis of what is going on in Othello's final speech and its further exposition of Othello's character is given by Jane Adamson:

Once we notice how transparent Othello's self-dramatizations are, we also recognize how crucially necessary they are to him: without them he could not survive.

Hence, they prompt us to a much more complex and disturbing judgement than Leavis's frowningly superior comment that Othello exhibits 'an attitude *towards* the emotion expressed – an attitude of a kind we are familiar with in the analysis of sentimentality' [*C*, pp. 131–2]. The 'sentimentality' is Othello's own, not Shakespeare's and what Shakespeare imaginatively grasps and dramatizes and makes us respond to are the vital reasons for, and the vital reality of, this man visibly straining *not* to recognize how idealizing and sentimental – indeed, how false – his extenuating self-images are. What we are dramatically shown is more than Othello's exhibition of 'an attitude towards the emotion expressed'. We are shown a desperate action: specifically Othello's effort to dull his emotions, even to replace them with 'attitudes', since he can neither express nor bear nor transform them in any other way. (1980, pp. 289)

Shakespeare, she argues, 'leaves open several ways for us to comprehend Othello's act of suicide' (p. 296).

His self-murder implies his final acknowledgement of what he has sometimes fleetingly recognized as the absolute ground of his emotional and moral life, but which another current of his being has always striven to master and deny: his absolute need for Desdemona's unalterable love . . . in this single act, he at once *acknowledges*, *accepts* and *cancels* that need and that impossibility forever. (p. 297)

A word or two must be devoted to the matter of Othello's jealousy. To Bradley, Othello's 'whole nature was indisposed to jealousy' and Othello himself remarks that he is not easily jealous. Others, such as Traversi, have asked, 'Who . . . has ever been more easily jealous than Othello?' (1956, p. 149). Stoll found inconsistency between the noble control exhibited by Othello in the first part of the play and his jealous mania of Act IV. Shakespeare's psychological shift was unconvincing (1915, pp. 21–3). Kenneth Muir neatly sums up these positions (1972, pp. 97–9) then draws on Lily B. Campbell's *Shakespeare's Tragic Heroes* (1961, pp. 148ff.) to suggest that it is Iago who is *the* jealous man, jealousy being 'one phase of envy', and he goes on to show the wide spread of jealousy within the play – in Bianca and Roderigo as well as Iago and Othello. It is Iago, says Muir, who 'infects Othello with his own jealousy' and that is shown by the transfer of imagery (1972, pp. 113–14). John Vyvyan suggested both characters were jealous: 'Iago is jealousy, and jealousy is the flaw in Othello's character' (1959, pp. 97–8).

The last word in this brief account of character and psychology in *Othello* ought to return the play to the theatre. Emrys Jones rightly points out that

> A solitary private reading of *Othello* may leave one feeling curiously unsure about Othello's reality as a person – he may seem less solidly realised than the heroes of some of the other tragedies. . . . But . . . in performance he seems to acquire an intense reality, which is clearly in part due to the mere fact of embodiment in the actor, but also seems due to certain qualities latent in the text which acting serves to bring out. These qualities are affective ones: for Shakespeare makes Othello . . . the focus for the readily available erotic feelings of the audience, its desire to bestow affection on one or more of the persons on the stage . . . in a performance we feel Othello's reality in the fact that it is he who at first provokingly resists our wishes and then indulges them, for no one else on stage has the power, as he has, to give this specifically dramatic pleasure.   (*ShS 21*, pp. 130–1)

The great Russian director and co-founder with Stanislavski of the Moscow Arts Theatre, Nemirovich-Danchenko (1859–1943), said that 'the main thing about Othello is the integrity and complete trustfulness of this great child. The actor who will be able to convince the audience of this will be giving the true Shakespeare.' It was this precept that informed the performance of Othello by one of the leading Soviet actors in the 1930s, Alexander Ostuzhev (1874–1953). He played Othello, 'not as a drama of jealousy but as a tragedy of trust deceived . . . an interpretation . . . remarkable for its humanism' (Samarin and Nikolyukin, 1966, p. 270).

The play as dramatic poem

Those critics who have treated Shakespeare's plays as if they were poems have in recent years been themselves the object of adverse criticism. Some of this has been touched on earlier in this study. When F. R. Leavis considers it 'necessary to insist' that *Othello* 'is poetic drama' and not a psychological novel, no one can demur, but a certain doubt may creep in when he equates 'poetic drama' directly with 'a dramatic poem'. These forms are not synonymous. From the Lindisfarne 'Harrowing of Hell' of the eighth century to Browning's dramatic monologues and beyond, the dramatic poem has been a distinct genre. Drama, poetic or not, as its root meaning implies, is unlike a dramatic poem in demanding enactment, physical embodiment. This uneasy relationship of the poetic and dramatic informs Leavis's argument elsewhere. Thus, when relating Bradley's 'obtuseness to the tragic significance' of *Othello*, and his 'insensibility' to Shakespeare's poetry, Leavis insidiously slips in parenthetically a rather doubtful assertion: 'it is still not superfluous to insist that the poetic skill is one with the dramatic' (*C*, p. 137). Muir, referring to Leavis on Othello's final speech, explains Leavis's shortcomings thus:

> It looks as though a prejudice against the theatre and a failure to realise the necessities of the stage have led Dr Leavis into confusing dramatisation with its necessary projection of character and the self-dramatisation of characters in real life. In his essay on the sentimentalist's Othello he was not merely disagreeing with Bradley but with three hundred years of stage tradition.   (1972, p. 103)

Because Leavis's essay has been so influential, and because he was a remarkable critic of poetry and the novel, he tends to be picked out as if he were the only one to regard drama as poetry. But he was in good company. G. R. Elliott, in his detailed, scene-by-scene, study of *Othello*, concludes his Introduction with, '*Othello* is Shakespeare's, and surely the world's, supreme *secular* tragic poem of "human love divine"' (1953, p. xxxiv, adapting Milton's poetic image, 'Human face divine'). R. A. Foakes in 'Suggestions for a New Approach to Shakespeare's Imagery' prefaced his proposals by referring to L. C. Knight's plea in 1933 that 'the only profitable approach to Shakespeare is a consideration of his plays as dramatic poems', and A. H. Sackton's 1948 statement in his *Rhetoric as a Dramatic Language in Ben Jonson*, that 'it is now becoming a commonplace of criticism that an Elizabethan play may be approached most profitably not as a study of human character, or as an expression of individual philosophy, but as a dramatic poem'. As Foakes put it, 'the plea of 1933 has now become a commonplace' (1952, p. 81). E. A. M. Colman parodied the title of another influential approach to drama as dramatic poem – C. S. Lewis's 1942 lecture '*Hamlet*: The Prince or the Poem?' – in a short study of this phenomenon, '*Hamlet*: The Poem or the Play?' He commented upon the concept of the play as dramatic poem thus:

As a way of alerting readers of a Shakespearian tragedy to its metaphoric life, its reverberating power, such a half-truth as this could once be tolerated, but in the forty-odd years since it was first offered our awareness of the category 'drama' has grown wider. Where critics in the 1930s and 1940s were content to lump in verse-dramas with all the other long poems they knew, we nowadays have to insist [*that word again!*] that the words on the page are not everything when it comes to this particular art-form. We have learned to give detailed attention to theatrical elements that cannot be accounted for entirely in terms of how 'the poem' works.   (1975–6, p. 4)

He concludes his essay with a succinct summary of his position: 'the poem is part of a larger whole' (p. 12). Helen Gardner illustrated this argument by tellingly quoting Ezra Pound: 'The medium of drama is not words, but persons moving about on a stage using words' (*C*, p. 149).

As one who is very much of the drama rather than the play-as-poem party, that must represent my position. On the other hand, it is not difficult to see why L. C. Knights should argue in 1933 in a famous essay, 'How Many Children had Lady Macbeth?' that 'the only profitable approach to Shakespeare is a consideration of his plays as dramatic poems' rather than in the more easily extractable elements of 'plot' and 'character' (1964, p. 18), even if we should not now take this for granted. And it is proper to point out that the word 'poem' could – and to Shakespeare – mean a play. It is, perhaps, used in that way by G. R. Elliott above. Indeed, its use can be extended to life itself. In the texts of all Shakespeare's work the word 'poem' occurs only once. In *Hamlet*, II.ii, Polonius speaks of the touring theatricals who are to visit Elsinore. He describes them as the best actors in the world for all kinds of absurdly categorised genres of drama, including 'poem unlimited'. Here 'poem' means play (one that ignores the unities), although put into the mouth of Polonius it might be suspect. But no one can doubt Ben Jonson's usage in the adulatory poem preceding Shakespeare's collected plays published in 1623 (the poems are not included). Jonson calls Shakespeare 'Star of Poets' and adduces that 'a good Poet's made, as well as borne'. Jonson is plainly referring to Shakespeare as dramatist. Whether that is *quite* the same as saying, as does Harold Goddard, 'that Shakespeare is primarily a poet ought to be so obvious that even to put the thought in words would be banal' (1960, p. viii), is not so certain, but it points us in a very important direction and one, in the thirties, given less attention than was justified. In passing, 'poetry' could be used 'to the life'. Jonson again: writing of his son's early death he movingly called him 'Ben Jonson, his best piece of poetry'. So, although it can lead to misunderstanding and partial interpretation if a play is considered as a dramatic poem – as a poem on a page – there is justification for regarding Shakespeare's tragedies as poems and the dramatist Shakespeare as poet.

An important technique in the examination of a play as poem, and one that can give enlightenment as to its dramatic nature, is the study of the poem's imagery. Images, their recurrence and their association with particular characters or aspects of a play can be most revealing. As Northrop Frye explains,

> formal criticism . . . is commentary, and commentary is the process of translating into explicit or discursive language what is implicit in the poem. Good commentary naturally does not read ideas into the poem; it reads and translates what is there, and the evidence that it is there is offered by the

study of the structure of imagery with which it begins.   (1957, p. 86)

Thus, in *Antony and Cleopatra*, images of soft and luxurious living contrast with those of hardness and military life to represent (and this is putting it crudely) Egypt and Rome and the erotic strengths and weaknesses of Cleopatra and Antony; Macbeth's clothes are too big for him, indicating he is a usurper: 'Now does he feel his title / Hang loose about him, like a giant's robe / Upon a dwarfish thief' [*Macbeth*, v.ii.20–2]. Caroline Spurgeon, in her pioneering study *Shakespeare's Imagery and What It Tells Us* (1935), pointed to (and illustrated) the contrasts of black and white in *Othello* (p. 64); images of sin and evil as 'foul, black, stained and filthy' – 'So will I turn her virtue into pitch' [II.iii.365] (p. 159); and the frequency with which the stench of sin and evil is brought before us – 'Villainy, villainy, villainy! / I think upon't: I think: I smell't: O villainy!' [v.ii.190–1] (p. 162); but, she says,

> The main image in *Othello* is that of animals in action, preying upon one another, mischievous, lascivious, cruel or suffering, and through these, the general sense of pain and unpleasantness is much increased and kept constantly before us.
>
> More than half the animal images in the play are Iago's, and all these are contemptuous or repellent . . . .   (p. 335)

The individualisation of characters through their imagery was taken further in 1949 by Mikhail Morozov and he paid particular attention to Othello, Iago and Desdemona. S. L. Bethell's study of diabolic imagery (discussed under 'Historical and social criticism') takes this approach further still and shows how imagery can open up an important dimension of the play, 'reading and translating what is there'. It is easy to see why L. C. Knights should argue that 'the essential structure of the plays is . . . in the poetry' and it requires only the change of the first 'the' to 'an' for even the most stage-oriented critic to agree. The interrelation of aspects of the play in which the quality of the language is given prominence is to be found in Helen Gardner's 'The Noble Moor':

Among the tragedies of Shakespeare *Othello* is supreme in one quality: beauty. Much of its poetry, in imagery, perfection of phrase, and steadiness of rhythm, soaring yet firm, enchants the sensuous imagination. . . . But *Othello* is also remarkable for another kind of beauty. . . . The play has a rare intellectual beauty, satisfying the desire of the imagination for order and harmony between the parts and the whole. Finally, the play has intense moral beauty. It makes an immediate appeal to the moral imagination, in its presentation in the figure of Desdemona of a love that does not alter. . . . These three kinds of beauty are interdependent, since all arise from the nature of the hero. (*C*, p. 147)

Wilson Knight considered 'the matter of style . . . crucial' in an interpretation of *Othello*. The qualities which distinguished it from other Shakespearian poetry were as follows:

It holds a rich music all its own, and possesses a unique solidity and precision of picturesque phrase or image, a peculiar chastity and serenity of thought. It is, as a rule, barren of direct metaphysical content. Its thought does not mesh with the reader's: rather it is always outside us, aloof. This aloofness is the resultant of an inward aloofness of image from image, word from word. The dominant quality is separation, not, as is more usual in Shakespeare, cohesion. (*C*, p. 73)

In addition to this separation, he points later to 'the tremendous reversal from extreme, almost over-decorative, beauty, to extreme ugliness – both of a kind unusual in Shakespeare' and that reflects 'a primary truth about the play'. '*Othello* is built rather of outstanding differences. . . . Instead of reading a unique, pervading, atmospheric suggestion – generally our key to interpretation of what happens within that atmosphere – we must here read the meaning of separate persons', especially the 'vividly separate' Othello, Desdemona and Iago (*C*, p. 80). Othello's 'slightly strained emotionalism' means that he 'often just misses tragic dignity' but Iago's seeming victory is not complete. Unlike some other thirties' critics, Wilson Knight sees Othello in the final scene as a nobly tragic figure. His ravings are not final: he rises beyond them. He slays Desdemona finally not so much in rage, as for 'the cause' (v.ii.1). He slays her in love. . . . At the end we know that Othello's fault is simplicity alone. . . . His simple faith in himself endures . . . .

This is indicated by the imagery, especially the 'symbols of the wide beauty of the universe [which] enrich his thoughts' (*C*, p. 95).

Robert B. Heilman has put well the interaction of the play as poem and the play as enacted stage drama:

If love is what *Othello* is 'about', *Othello* is not only a play about love but a poet about love. [In his footnotes he here quotes Elmer Stoll: 'a tragedy which is also a poem, in which the parts "mutually support and explain each other"'.] It has parts which interact in the mode of 'pure' drama – people having such and such an effect on each other, irrespective of whether they communicate in verse, prose, or pantomime; it also has parts which interact in the manner of a poem. . . . Yet when the dramatist has his characters speak in poetic language, he vastly complicates their communication with each other and with us. Figure, rhythm, poetic order do not merely make 'more vivid' or 'heighten' a literal prose statement that is otherwise unchanged; they constitute a fundamentally different statement by the introduction of the nuance, overtone, feeling, association, implication, and extension characteristic of them . . . .   (1956, p. 3)

A little later he quotes from Wolfgang Clemen's *The Development of Shakespeare's Imagery* in support of the argument that in the tragedies 'the images become "an inherent part of the dramatic structure", resembling "a second line of action . . . and providing a 'counterpoint' to the events on the stage"' (p. 7).

The matter of what a work is 'about' (and Heilman is careful to place this idea by putting the word about in quotation marks), demands a brief word of comment. Northrop Frye succinctly summed up this 'central dilemma of literature' in 'The Road of Excess': 'If literature is didactic, it tends to injure its own integrity; if it ceases wholly to be didactic, it tends to injure its own seriousness.' He quotes Shelley's 'Didactic poetry is my abhorrence' but argues that 'if the main body of Shelley's poetry had not been directly concerned with social, moral, religious, philosophical, political issues he would have lost most of his self-respect as a poet' (1963, p. 14).

There can be little doubt that the most remarkable study of poetic language in *Othello* is the analysis of the use of 'honest' in William Empson's *The Structure of Complex Words*. There is an extract from this book in the *Casebook* on *Othello*, but it is a critical exercise that needs to be read in the full context of its source. Interestingly, he remarks that his consideration of the language dated after seeing a performance of *Othello* which featured 'a particularly good Iago'. He did not think about the implications of 'honest' at the time of the performance. His verbal analysis followed from an examination of the text to see to what extent it supported his impressions of the play: 'But I do not feel this to be any reason for doubting that the puns on *honesty* really do support [those impressions]' (*C*, p. 122).

Empson analyses the fifty-two uses of 'honest' and 'honesty' in *Othello* (there are, in fact, fifty-six). He argues that the word was changing in its meaning – or rather its implication – and that Shakespeare sensed this process. 'What Shakespeare hated in the word, I believe, was a peculiar use, at once hearty and individualist, which was then common among raffish low people but did not become upper-class until the Restoration' (p. 98). Shakespeare 'never once allows the word a simple hearty use between equals' (p. 99). It is impossible to extract the argument in all its subtlety, but a couple of lines of a single quotation analysed by Empson may indicate the kind of paradox to which he was drawing attention: Iago's, 'O wretched fool, / That lov'st to make thine honesty, a vice!' [III.iii.376] (Empson capitalises 'honesty' and 'vice', so 'Vice' has the sense of wickedness and the Fool of the morality plays). Empson's close analysis shows how there is little that is 'simple honest' about the use of this word, and how its use affects – infects – the whole play, for it helps dupe those in the audience as well as those on stage. All the elements of Iago's character 'are represented in the range of meanings of *honest* . . . the confusion of moral theory in the audience, which would make them begin by approving of Iago . . . was symbolised or echoed in a high degree by the confusion of the word' (*C*, p. 122).

Archetypal criticism

There are more distinctive critical approaches than can
conveniently be focused upon in a study of less than
voluminous proportions. This selection attempts simply to
suggest a number of ways that might be helpful to the study of
Othello. Rather than touch upon it indirectly under other heads
(as here under 'Historical and social criticism'), there are
clearly possibilities for a thoroughgoing Christian approach.
Because so much critical attention has been concentrated upon
Othello and Iago, Desdemona has received scant justice, and,
although an attempt will be made in Part Two to remedy that, a
feminist approach would doubtless have presented a different
balance. Marxist criticism would also have offered a distinctive
way of looking at *Othello*. One excellent example of such an
approach, G. M. Matthews's '*Othello* and the Dignity of Man',
has been referred to at the end of the section devoted to
historical and social criticism. The approaches of semiologists,
structuralists and deconstructivists might all have been given
attention. Indeed, Roland Barthes's long essay, 'Myth Today',
which did much to bring semiological criticism to a wide
audience, contains an analysis of an image that has a peculiarly
revealing relevance to *Othello* – to Othello indeed. Barthes
describes how he saw a copy of *Paris-Match* in a barber-shop.
The cover featured 'a young Negro in a French uniform . . .
saluting, with his eyes uplifted, probably fixed on a fold of the
tricolour', France's national flag (1973, p. 116). This has many
implications. The 'signs' betoken a complex of attitudes and
emotions. Is 'colour' shown here without racial discrimination?
Does such loyalty to the empire of France deny colonialism?
Does it suggest a greater patriotism? What is the relationship of
the black soldier, 'with eyes uplifted', to white authority?
What, indeed, can be read into – or read *from* – 'with eyes
uplifted'? Shakespeare's dramatic representation of such and
other related issues in *Othello* is infinitely more complicated
than those arising from such a 'simple' image, but from the kind
of analysis that Barthes made of that cover of *Paris-Match* there
is much that would illuminate *Othello*.
   Implicit in a discussion of what this illustration signifies are
deep-seated responses and attitudes which may be at work
subconsciously in the beholder, attitudes which may be

explained by an understanding of myth. Barthes uses the word 'myth' in a particular way. For him, 'myth is a type of speech. . . . Myth is not defined by the object of its message, but by the way in which it utters this message.' To illustrate that it is not the object that defines myth but the way in which it is represented he notes,

> A tree is a tree. . . . But a tree as expressed by Minou Drouet is no longer quite a tree, it is a tree which is decorated, adapted to a certain type of consumption [i.e. designed for a particular audience], laden with literary self-indulgence, revolt, images, in short with a type of social *usage* which is added to pure matter.   (1973, p. 109)

Perhaps more broadly relevant to *Othello* is myth as used in an earlier sense: the kind of myth which explains 'origin and eventual extinction', which answers 'the sort of awkward questions that children ask, such as "Who made the world? How will it end?" . . .', and which can 'justify an existing social system and account for traditional rites and customs' (Robert Graves, Introduction to *Larousse Encyclopaedia of Mythology*, 1959, p. v). Such myths, it has been argued, can be related to subconscious aspects of our lives and characters. They form part of a common stock of experience which may prompt, say, an audience at a play to respond to what is presented to them even though they are individually unaware of what, subconsciously, generates that response.

Interest in myth and ritual was prompted especially by Sir James Frazer's twelve-volume work *The Golden Bough* (1890–1915) and Jane Harrison's *Ancient Art and Ritual* (1917). It was effectively taken further by Jesse Watson in *From Ritual to Romance* (1920 – a source of T. S. Eliot's *The Waste Land*), and in the stimulating if controversial *The Origin of Attic Comedy* (1914) by F. M. Cornford, which initiated the scholarly and more important *Dithyramb, Tragedy and Comedy* (1927) by A. W. Pickard-Cambridge. To examinations of myth in its own right and in its relation to the foundations of drama (applications which are only riskily overlooked, whatever other critical approaches are followed) was then joined a concept that underpins the archetypal approach: Jung's theory of the collective unconscious. This was handily explained by Wilbur Scott:

> civilised man preserves, though unconsciously, those prehistorical areas of knowledge which he articulated obliquely in myth. If valid, the speculation explains the somewhat mysterious appeal of mythical stories long after the supernatural elements in them have ceased to command belief. (1962, p. 248)

(Scott's introductions to each of the five approaches he selects, the moral, psychological, sociological, formalist and archetypal, will all be helpful to those using this book, and the essays chosen to demonstrate the approaches – two of which are devoted to *As You Like It* and 'Hamlet and Orestes' – are illuminating.)

There can be little doubt that the power of *Othello* in the theatre is in part to be explained by this appeal to the collective unconscious. It is possible also that the peculiar viciousness that animates some critics of *Othello*, towards Othello and towards critics with whom they disagree, may stem from what in *Othello* subconsciously disturbs them. The sense of personal affront that seems to be experienced may be the manifestation of that deep-seated unease which the play prompts in them. The 'purist critic' looks at the work of the 'sentimentalist critic' (I use quotation marks to draw attention to a deliberate crudity of categorisation), and finds it wanting. He resorts to denigration of the characters and insult of the rival critics. Looking at it dispassionately we may well agree with much of the analysis of the 'purist', yet somehow the 'sentimentalist' *Othello* strikes home to us. Dramatic convention, physical embodiment, stage positioning, beauty of rhythm and language may all play a part in making the play work far, far more effectively than, for some critics, it seems to have any right so to do. It is not difficult to see Hamlet and Orestes as 'traditional types' (as Gilbert Murray does in the essay reprinted by Scott), but does the dramatic vitality of *Othello*, which *is* unquestioned, stem from its appeal to something deep within us? Has it some archetypal power? Is it touching on suppressed emotions, conflicts, fears? If that is so (and I think it

may be), is it that which makes the play so very effective in the
theatre (when emotion might be said to rule) and which, in
touching what a critic in his study is unable to recognise within
his subconscious, vents itself forth in personal spite? I propose,
therefore, to look at two aspects of the archetypal approach.
First, one of the studies that has achieved a classic status,
Archetypal Patterns in Poetry: Psychological Studies of Imagination by
Maud Bodkin (even though her approach does not overimpress
so good a scholar as Dame Helen Gardner – see *C*, p. 97 n. 5);
and Northrop Frye's *Anatomy of Criticism*.

Leah Scragg, near the end of her essay 'Iago – Vice or Devil?'
(referred to under 'Dramatic convention and decorum'), writes
of Iago as akin to 'the archetypal adversary of mankind' as
repeated over and over again in Christian literature (*ShS 21*,
p. 64). 'Archetypal' implies more than, say, 'traditional': Iago
is not simply filling a traditional role. The archetypal goes
much deeper. Maud Bodkin starts her book by summarising
something Carl Jung wrote in his article 'On the Relation of
Analytical Psychology to Poetic Art' in 1928:

> The special emotional significance possessed by certain
> poems – a significance going beyond any definite meaning
> conveyed – he attributes to the stirring in the reader's mind,
> within or beneath his conscious response, of unconscious
> forces which he terms 'primordial images', or archetypes.
> These archetypes he describes as 'psychic residua of
> numberless experiences of the same type', experiences which
> have happened not to the individual but to his ancestors, and
> of which the results are inherited in the structure of the brain,
> *a priori* determinants of individual experience.   (1934, p. 1)

In her second appendix she refers to Stoll's censure of those
who confuse poetic drama with psychological documents. She
respects his argument (outlined under 'Dramatic convention
and decorum') that 'the "independent" condition of Othello's
mind and the "impenetrableness" of Iago's mask, are elements
in a dramatic convention' (p. 332). However, she argues that
her approach is not, in fact, a psychological analysis of Othello
(or Hamlet), nor of Shakespeare, but one 'of the experience
communicated to ourselves when we live in the art of the play'
(p. 333) – that is, especially at a performance. Three quotations

might give some impression of what this approach may reveal.
First,

> If we attempt to define the devil in psychological terms,
> regarding him as an archetype . . . we may say that devil is
> our tendency to represent in personal form the forces within
> and without us that threaten our supreme values.   (p. 223)

As to Iago's 'honesty' she remarks,

> Iago seems to Othello so honest, so wise beyond himself in
> human dealings, possessed of a terrible power of seeing and
> speaking truth, because into what he speaks are projected the
> half truths that Othello's romantic vision ignored, but of
> which his mind held secret knowledge.   (p. 223)

(Here she refers to Othello's 'mind' as a shorthand way of
expressing the complex relationship outlined in her second
appendix, referred to above.) This devil-figure of Iago

> gathers into himself forces inherent in Othello and in the
> heroic world he represents. Iago is the shadow-side of
> Othello, the devil-shape that the resistant clay, 'moving
> awry', generates from the imposition of that too single-
> hearted ideal which Othello as hero represents.

Thus, she says, Othello, Hamlet and Lear, like Milton's Satan,
found 'around him and deep within himself, devilish enmity
and betrayal, and was . . . "hurled headlong" to individual
ruin' (p. 245).

Part One of this little book concludes with a very brief
introduction to a stimulating, controversial and demanding
approach, that of Northrop Frye's *Anatomy of Criticism*. Frye
makes little reference to *Othello*, and his most significant *aperçu*
with regard to the play has already been noted under 'Genre
criticism'. Frye challenges all approaches based on value-
judgements:

> Value-judgements are subjective in the sense that they can
> be indirectly but not directly communicated. When they are
> fashionable or generally accepted, they look objective, but

that is all. . . . every new critical fashion, such as the current fashion for elaborate rhetorical analysis, has been accompanied by a belief that criticism has finally devised a definitive technique for separating the excellent from the less excellent. But this always turns out to be an illusion of the history of taste. (1957, p. 20)

What is more, he says, rhetorical value-judgements 'are closely related to social values, and are usually cleared through a customs-house of moral metaphors: sincerity, economy, subtlety, simplicity, and the like' (p. 21). Thus, 'the critic is thrown back on prejudice derived from his existence as a social being' (p. 22). Frye is not alone in expressing dissatisfaction with literary criticism as it is customarily practised. Feminists have reacted against male-oriented criticism, and an advocate of structuralism and semiotics has been described by James Gribble as seeking something that will replace what is for this academic a discredited form of criticism 'which was merely an ideological outgrowth of capitalism, prizing those values of a decaying aristocracy which are characteristically revered by a sycophantic middle class' (1983, p. 90). To Frye, 'All efforts of critics to discover rules or laws in the sense of telling the artist what he ought to do, or have done, to be an authentic artist, have failed.' And he quotes Shelley: 'Poetry, and the art which professes to regulate and limit its powers, cannot subsist together' (p. 26). He therefore offers, with philosophic, quasi-scientific, rigour, a highly schematic approach based on archetypes of all literature of all periods. There are four essays devoted to theories of modes, symbols, myths and genres, each being concerned respectively with historical, ethical, archetypal and rhetorical criticism. Brief mention (which can do little justice to Frye's range of literary reference and intellectual depth) will be made to the first and third essays, beginning with 'Archetypal Criticism: Theory of Myths'.

Archetypally, says Frye, 'tragedy [is] a *mimesis* of sacrifice' (p. 214). He identifies six 'phases' of tragedy (pp. 214–23). These move from the heroic to the ironic. Frye does not relate these to *Othello* (he gives other illustrations), so the parallels that follow are mine. In the first phase 'the central character is given the greatest possible dignity in contrast to the other characters'; the dignity of Othello's first appearance, his dialogue with Brabantio, and his speech to the Senators are obvious. In the second phase, the hero is dominated by the loss of innocence, he is baffled, and there is a loss of that native simplicity which arises from a lack of worldly wisdom; again, a process very plain in Othello as Iago's poison begins to work. In the third phase there is emphasis on the success or completeness of the hero's achievement: how successful has been the marriage of Othello and Desdemona?

The tragic wheel turns downwards with the fourth phase as the hero crosses the boundary line from innocence to experience – the scales seem to be stripped from Othello's eyes. In the penultimate phase the ironic begins to dominate the heroic. The hero is placed 'in a state of lower freedom than the audience'. Othello, who once exercised authority, is now manipulated; ironically, one not easily jealous becomes frenziedly so; Othello's actions are so constrained that a tragic outcome is inevitable. Finally, in the sixth phase, the hero archetypally enters a world of shock and horror in which the central images include mutilation and torture – Othello's anguished and tortured spirit finds release only in his self-mutilation as he plunges his knife into himself. 'At the end of this phase we reach a point of demonic epiphany, where we see or glimpse the undisplaced demonic vision, the vision of the *Inferno*.'

This progression of phases, Frye argues, is common to all tragedy – hence their archetypal nature. In his discussion of the theory of modes (pp. 33–67), Frye delineates five categories. Some works will be wholly, or mainly, in one mode. The first, the *mythic mode*, features superhuman characters who are not bound by the laws of natural order. The Homeric epics are in this mode, but elements may appear in other tragedies – in *Othello* in such lines as 'Against all rules of nature' [I.iii.101]. The second mode is *romance*, a world of wonder in which there will be elements of supernatural power – as in the stories of King Arthur and Excalibur. *Othello* is rich with such elements. Bradley, it will be recalled, described Othello as belonging not to our world; 'he seems to enter it we know not whence – almost as if from a wonderland' (*C*, p. 58) and there are many, many references to charms, magic, drugs, bewitchment and the world of wonders (the Anthropophagi, for instance). In the *high mimetic mode*, the hero is natural man but 'head and shoulders above others', often a ruler; Othello is a military commander and Shakespeare seems to go to some trouble to have Othello descend from 'men of royal siege' [I.ii.22]. The *low mimetic mode* presents a world such as we might live in – Othello's hopes and fears are as our own. Finally, in the *ironic mode* the hero is looked down upon; Othello becomes the fool of love (he triply calls himself 'fool' at v.ii.319), a slave: he that was 'once so good' has 'Fallen in the practice of a damned slave' [v.ii.289–90].

Whereas in *Antony and Cleopatra* there is rich imagery relating the play to the mythic mode, and all five modes are reflected in that play, *Othello*, though there are mythic mode allusions, is far stronger in the other four modes and it is not difficult to see Othello move from the romantic–high mimetic modes to the low mimetic and ironic. Such an approach tells us something about the nature and qualities of *Othello* without depending upon value-judgements which may depend upon fashion, prejudice and whim. It is, however, only fair to quote David Lodge's comment that this highly schematic approach 'neglects the historical, particular, verbally unique aspects of literary artefacts, and that archetypal criticism, so far from being scientific, is neither verifiable nor falsifiable' (1972, p. 421).

Part Two
Appraisal

Contextual criticism

I DESCRIBE my approach as contextual. This is not a word I admire very much, but it does, I think, suggest that combination of the different critical milieux in which *Othello* may fruitfully be studied. I have in mind the social and historical context of the time when the play was written – either in the last months of the reign of Queen Elizabeth or, more probably, shortly after the accession of James I; the context of the play in performance, i.e. when embodied in physical action rather than read either without reference to the theatre or (still unsatisfactory) read 'in the theatre of the mind'; and the context of our own time and place. This does not mean that problems that are usually only apparent in the study will be ignored. Intelligent reading of text alone is important not only for the student, but ought to be the basis of the work of every actor and director. Paradoxically, I shall focus on one of the play's problems that is said to disappear in the theatre – double time. However, I shall think of this not as 'a problem for the study', 'an academic matter' (and 'academic' in our society is taken to mean, 'it doesn't matter'), but as part of the design of the play which Shakespeare might have expected the more perspicacious of his audience to spot.

I shall also give prominence to the matter of colour. I am not concerned with precisely what non-white colour Shakespeare had in mind for Othello – I think he is meant to be black – but am concerned with colour as a key to a full understanding of *Othello* and its impact upon us. I am well aware that there are eminent critics who deny that colour is at issue in *Othello*; I once thought that myself – or, rather, I too easily slipped into that assumption. I changed my mind some twenty years ago when, for the first time, I taught *Othello* to a group of a dozen students one of whom, and only one, was black. We all, students and teacher, white and black alike, fell backwards to avoid giving offence, to assure each other and ourselves that our liberal consciences were in harmony and our hearts beat, very visibly, in the right place. We all meant well and I recall no animosity or hurt. But there was an electricity at work in those seminars! I had not then read G. M. Matthews's '*Othello* and the Dignity of Man', and I am not a Marxist, but I find much to agree with in his argument demonstrating the relevance of the colour of our skins to this play, now *and in Shakespeare's time*. It is not something our present concerns inject into a late-twentieth-century reading of the play.

Shakespeare touches raw nerves in *Othello*: racial difference, sexual jealousy, and especially the very wonder of innocent love – can we face that without cynicism or disbelief? – innocent love corrupted by malice, envy, and *our* subconscious will that it be destroyed. Shakespeare dramatises characters tempted to hate and destroy rather than accept such a love, and, even more telling, he tempts his audiences to do the same. That is why *Othello* is so disturbing a play; that is why, I guess, it produces some pretty ugly criticism. Fortunately, in the theatre, such is Shakespeare's artistry, though we witness the destruction of that which is the most precious human relationship, even subconsciously willing it on like a crowd watching violence at a soccer ground or poring over its replay on a television screen, we are also enabled to purge something of that will to destruction within us as we see Othello destroy himself. Of all Shakespeare's tragedies, *Othello* most involves the audience as a whole and individually in its torments and resolution. Because at our best we can aspire to selfless love, but fear the despoilments of envy and jealousy, and are shamed by the rejection of other human beings, we can respond most intimately to this play. At its end we cannot rejoice in storms weathered or content ourselves with the thought of a bright new world dawning, but we can understand, and be emotionally satisfied by, the tragic outcome of the pure love that briefly united Othello and Desdemona. In the theatre there is a kind of exorcism of something deep within us, something possibly outside the experience of a study-bound reading.

Leslie Fiedler, in *An End of Innocence* (1952), touches on an aspect of American literature which, despite its very different field of reference, hints at something that underlies the unease properly invoked by *Othello*:

> It is perhaps to be expected that the Negro and the homosexual should become stock literary themes in a period when the exploration of responsibility and failure has become again a primary concern of our literature. It is the discrepancy they represent that haunts us, that moral discrepancy before which we are helpless, having no resources (no tradition of courtesy, no honored mode of cynicism) for dealing with a conflict of principle and practice. (Scott, 1962, p. 303)

The text

The second syllable of 'contextual' points to an important and intractable aspect of the context in which we read *Othello* or upon which a performance is based: the text. What authority have the words we say or read? It is reasonable to imagine that a text of a work will always be the same, bar an occasional misprint, unless the author revises or the censor cuts. That is not so. As the little example given at the end of the Introduction shows, readings vary even between contemporary texts, and they may even involve the silent omission of sentences, paragraphs, pages. *Othello* exists in two markedly different versions. One is an edition of the play printed in its own right in 1622 (the First Quarto) and the other is that included in Shakespeare's collected plays published in 1623 (the First Folio). There is no agreement as to how these different versions arose in the two decades between publication and the first recorded performance on 1 November 1604 at King James's court, nor can their relationship be explained satisfactorily. The First Folio has some 160 lines not in the Quarto; the Quarto has phrases and over fifty oaths not in the Folio; and there are about a thousand verbal differences between the two texts. Only the more scholarly modern editions have space to record these differences accurately and to give some account of the textual theories which try to explain what happened. What is certain is that any edition used for study of acting will

(1) differ from other editions, often crucially; and (2) be a conflation of the two different versions. These may derive from a single Shakespeare manuscript, or from two versions both by Shakespeare.

Thus, when interpreting Othello's final speech, it is important to realise that Othello might be comparing himself to 'the base Indian' who threw away a pearl (i.e. an ignorant native), or to 'the base Judean' – 'the' is important (Judas's betrayal of Christ or, less probably, Herod's rejection of his wife). Depending on how the texts evolved, Shakespeare could have been responsible for both readings; they could derive from a misreading by a scribe making a second manuscript; or from an error made by the man who set the type of one edition – though which must then be worked out. And this is but one of those many, many differences. Close critical analysis demands awareness of the textual stability of what is being analysed.

Racial difference

Bradley, in a passage immediately preceding the section quoted in the *Casebook*, went out of his way to dismiss at some length 'a mistaken view . . . that the play is primarily a study of a noble barbarian, who has become a Christian and has imbibed some of the civilisation of his employers, but who retains beneath the surface the savage passions of his Moorish blood' (1904, p. 186). Race, he admits, affects 'our idea' of Othello and 'makes a difference to the action and catastrophe', but, 'in regard to the essentials of his character', race is not important. In a slightly involved inverse way he then argues that an Englishman would have been as much a victim as this Moor in these circumstances (pp. 186–7). Bradley's desire to respond to race in a humane manner does him credit and it probably represents, even today, a very widespread desire. But, as G. M. Matthews points out, there is a revealing footnote later in that lecture. Bradley argues that the Moor is brown rather than black but admits that, if we were presented with a 'coal-black' Othello, 'the aversion of our blood . . . would overpower our imagination' (p. 202). This may well get to the heart of a deep-seated emotion which is very widespread. And it is, I believe, that emotion that Shakespeare is dramatising. In that same footnote there is a perhaps even more revealing comment. Bradley says, 'We do not like the real Shakespeare. We like to have his language pruned and his conceptions flattened into something that suits our mouths and minds.' We have, since Bradley wrote, learned to like his language to the full, but the conceptions may still be 'flattened', as I believe they are in most responses to *Othello*.

There are, oversimplifying, only two ways of considering the implications of Othello being black: it is irrelevant or it is, as I think G. M. Matthews has convincingly demonstrated, deeply significant. As has been mentioned under 'Historical and social criticism', there are quite a number of characters who are black in Elizabethan drama. By and large, when not actually bad, they are represented as 'lesser breeds without the Law', and so, in Shakespeare, Aaron, Caliban and the Prince of Morocco, whom Portia (epitome of Justice) bids adieu with 'A gentle riddance. . . . Let all of his complexion choose me so' (i.e. vainly). The folk tradition of opposing St George with a far-fetched alien character often specifically designated 'black' and associated with the Prince of Darkness directly or implicitly cannot but have been influential in Shakespeare's time, and, from what has been explained earlier, there was prejudice against blacks in the sixteenth century. Shakespeare always modified the stories he used. For *Othello*, he could easily have made his hero white, or stressed the lightness of his complexion, which would have given his hero an exotic touch, enough to intrigue audiences. That might have been a lesser dramatist's response. But Shakespeare follows a different course. He insists upon the blackness of his hero; it is drawn attention to in straightforward description and in deliberately disgusting images. What is more, the idea of blackness is driven home by the imagery of the play and (more obvious in our artificially-lit theatres than on open stages such as the Globe) by the darkness in which the play opens and closes. I don't see how a contemporary audience in Britain, America or a number of other countries can fail to bring into the theatre attitudes derived from their own innate responses to race. To pretend otherwise is to ally oneself with that silly lady from Maryland who always imagined Othello as white. The marriage of a middle-aged black man and a young white girl must, then and now, touch sensitive nerves in black and white. The effects of four centuries of colonialism (as Matthews mentions) might modify our responses, but they perhaps do no more than stand surrogate for folk-play memories now lost to us.

It is a short and false step from this to say the play is 'about' racial tension. It isn't. As Arthur Miller, with his play *The Crucible* in mind, succinctly put it, 'Before a play can be "about" something else, it has to be about itself' (1978, p. 295). The 'itself' within the play is that Othello, of royal descent, who comes before us 'dark and grand' in Bradley's phrase, trusted, able, Christian, respected, at the pinnacle of his service, can, when it comes to a crisis, be seen in loathsome terms by characters within the play – not merely Iago, but even such as Brabantio, who tells Othello that Desdemona faces ridicule because she has 'Run from her guardage to the sooty bosom / Of such a thing as thou' [I.ii.70–1]. *Othello* is not 'about' race, or colour, or even jealousy. It dramatises the way actions are directed rather by attitudes, fears and delusions that rule the subconscious than by evident facts. Thus, can (avoiding colour itself) Othello the princely commander suddenly become 'such a thing as thou' – a thing? The potent strength of *Othello* lies in its power to tap responses deep within the hearts of audiences, responses that, consciously, they might prefer to deny. Apart from the pervasive opposition of black and white throughout the play and the use of diabolic images, it is notable how Shakespeare prods the minds of his first audiences in a way that the passage of time has dimmed for us.

It has already been pointed out that Othello's name implies Ottoman, the force that presented the main challenge to Christian Europe in Shakespeare's time. His name is a frequent reminder of that threat, and 'Ottoman' itself occurs once, and 'Ottomites' three times. But there is a suggestion, made explicit by Iago, that the action concerns 'an erring barbarian and a super-subtle Venetian' [I.iii.343]. The smear is obvious; as 'fact' it is absurd. Venetians were reputedly sophisticated; Desdemona is a Venetian – so a young girl not long out of school becomes super-subtle and prejudice is fed, just as in a modern newspaper story about prominent people. But Othello is called an *erring* barbarian. He might loosely be described as 'from Barbary' – i.e. from that part of North Africa where the Berbers lived – and it is for Mauretania (whence 'Moor' is derived) that he and Desdemona are bound after Cassio takes over as Governor [iv.ii.217]. But that he is 'a barbarian' (the word is not derived from 'Barbary') is plainly not so; his initial demeanour ('Keep up your bright swords, for the dew will rust them' [i.ii.59]) makes that plain. 'Erring', however, has two implications. In a sense, Othello is a wanderer and that is not particularly objectionable: he is a stranger. But it also implies that he is sinful, or even pagan (which he is not). In a curious way, familiar to us from journalism, a mixture of half-truth and lie confirms our prejudices. Are we to trust the facts presented to us or work by prejudices to which we will scarcely admit? Shakespeare uses 'Barbary' or 'barbarous' on four other occasions. At i.i.111 Iago taunts Brabantio with the accusation that his daughter is 'covered with a Barbary horse'; then at ii.iii.153, Othello is for a second time called to calm 'a barbarous brawl' and here come references to turning Turk, Ottomites, and Christian shame. By his actions here Othello is shown to be the very opposite of barbarian. Then, very subtly, come two references to Barbary by Desdemona when, at the beginning of iv.iii, her thoughts are on death. The willow song she sings had been sung by a maid of her mother's called, not Barbara (which is related to 'barbarian'), but 'Barbary'.

As so often in Elizabethan and Jacobean drama, and especially in this play, the audience is called upon to exercise judgement, to distinguish facts from its prejudices.

What has been said of race and colour applies in a somewhat similar way to the theme of jealousy in the play. A common error here is in focusing attention on Othello. What is important is not so much whether Othello is by nature jealous or easily moved to jealousy, or even the smear that he is racially inclined to jealousy, as that we realise that it is Iago who is the most deeply envious of characters, who is jealous of Cassio, envious of Othello's and Desdemona's love, jealous of his own 'reputation', and that we understand how trust can be destroyed and jealousy fill its place. This reversal is not uncommon in Shakespeare and was well described by Maynard Mack in 'The Jacobean Shakespeare'.

Mack shows how the heroes of Shakespeare's great tragedies begin 'hyperbolically', go through a reversal of their characteristics, and then make some slight recovery following a recognition of their error. Thus Macbeth, head and shoulders above others in battle, capable of wading through a field of blood, with a sword that 'smoked with bloody execution', hewing his opponents from 'the nave to the chops', becomes fearful of the sight of a little blood on a dagger, but recovers sufficiently to die fighting bravely if forlornly. Hamlet, who procrastinates, becomes a man of too-ready action. Othello is presented to us as calm, noble, a character of massive dignity, even imperturbability. In action, as a military commander and, as we see, in the petty squabbles of I.ii and II.iii, and in speech, especially in his address to the senators, he stands head and shoulders, physically and metaphorically, above all those about him. And he has a noble trustfulness. Worked on by Iago, mistrusting his responses (and we cannot doubt that the racial misunderstanding to be found in the Venetians is to be found in the reverse direction in Othello), his trust is converted to its opposite. Then, as recognition comes to him of the brutality to which he has stooped, of what he has lost, he recovers a little of his former dignity when he recalls that time long past when he struck a blow for a worthy cause. Support for this pattern is to be found in the way that the diabolic images, noted by S. L. Bethell, move from Iago's language into Othello's (see above, 'Dramatic convention and decorum'). From dominating Iago's speech in the first two acts, they come to dominate Othello's in the third and fourth acts, and, significantly, whereas in Act I, when he is at his 'purest' and most noble, Othello has no such images, in the last act, when Iago is revealed for what he is and for what he has effected, it is he who has no use for such damages.

The change is effected, of course, by Iago. His function in the play has been nowhere better summed up than by the American dramatist Arthur Miller, with reference to his own play *The Crucible*, a play concerned with the evil of witch-hunts old and contemporary.

> I believe now, as I did not conceive then [before writing the play], that there are people dedicated to evil in the world; that without their perverse example we should not know the good. Evil is not a mistake but a fact in itself. . . . I believe merely that, from whatever cause, a dedication to evil, not mistaking it for good, but knowing it as evil and loving it as evil, is possible in human beings who appear agreeable and normal. I think now that one of the hidden weaknesses of our

whole approach to dramatic psychology is our inability to face this fact – to conceive, in effect, of Iago. (1978, p. 158)

Character antithesis

Maynard Mack's description of the transformation of the tragic hero (especially when filled out in his essay) adequately illustrates the broad sweep of Othello's development, but it is not, of course, intended to account fully for the characters of the heroes individually. It is a commonplace that Shakespeare draws 'rounded' characters (though often that leads to an unthinking disparagement of other dramatists, and especially Jonson, who were employing a quite different kind of characterisation). It is to be expected, therefore, that characters will not be 'all of a piece'. Even such a seemingly epic hero as Henry V can be shown to have very human failings. In *Othello*, however, the characters seem to have characteristics which might well be described as antithetical. As Wilson Knight put it, 'The dominant quality [of *Othello*] is separation, not, as is more usual in Shakespeare, cohesion'; *Othello* is built of 'outstanding differences (*C*, pp. 73, 80). Thus also, in a crude way, Iago's 'honesty' is anything but; the faithful servant is traitorous; his white exterior masks a black soul; and so on. This is all rather obvious, but it is carried through more subtly in his language. For example, after Othello has fallen in an epileptic fit in iv.i, Iago's 'Work on, / My medicine, work!' inverts meaning: 'medicine' is poison.

Cassio, too, in a fairly simple way can be seen to be compounded of opposites. He cannot be without merit; Othello would hardly have chosen him had he been so, and, even if Othello had misjudged his character, it says much for the confidence others have in him that Venice should send letters appointing him Governor in place of Othello and, even after all has been revealed, that he should be confirmed in office at the end of the play. Yet he is flawed by his failure either to hold his liquor or to have the sense not to drink so much. When drunk he lacks self-control – the capacity to command – and there is a parallel between Cassio drunk and Othello victim of falling-sickness, although there is far more to be made of Othello's trance. For all his pleasantness, there is a suggestion of a possibly fatal weakness about him, so that our confidence in him is less secure than that of Venice. As he was known to Desdemona, it is possible he should be considered among 'The wealthy curlèd darlings of our nation' that Brabantio tells us Desdemona shunned [I.ii.68].

But it is in Desdemona and Othello that we witness the contrasting traits of character so strongly, and in Othello that we see them so much at war with one another. It is very easy, as critics have noted, to canonise Desdemona, a fate rather common to a number of Shakespeare's particularly appealing heroines. Desdemona, however, is made of stern stuff and not all her characteristics are quite so saintly. This is far from giving credence to Iago's insinuations. It implies, rather, that she is human. It is a little too easy to consider Desdemona as not much more than the object of Othello's love and the victim of his passion. This is ironic, for Desdemona's chief quality, I should say, is her independence (a characteristic not uncommon in a number of Shakespeare's female characters). She is no shy, reticent creature when it comes to standing up for herself before the senators of Venice. Consider that she is brought, at night, to speak for herself and Othello before an angry and distressed father. Her language is firm, temperate, and ingenious. When she says at I.iii.179ff., 'My noble father, / I do perceive here a divided duty . . . ', we hear also the voices of Portia in the courtroom at Venice and of Cordelia before her father. The calm logic is undeniably of a cool, intelligent, independent mind. But the penultimate line contains a word that takes her a little beyond that: 'So much I *challenge*' – she is staking a claim to her 'rights' and challenging her father that they *are* her rights.

This must take us back a little to how it is that this challenge has arisen, and here something less admirable about Desdemona is revealed. It is of much less significance nowadays (though it can still cause distress) if a young woman should suddenly and secretly disappear from home, marry and live with her husband without letting her family know where she is. To Shakespeare's first audiences this must have seemed remarkably remiss, even shocking. It could not be excused as a mere romantic elopement; this was a serious breach of decorum. Not only was Desdemona wrong here, but Othello's behaviour is astonishing. A modern audience may wonder at charges that Desdemona has been spirited away by magic, love-charms and witchcraft, but to an Elizabethan her action took some explaining and witchcraft must, paradoxically, have given a 'rational' explanation. It is noticeable, too, how Shakespeare has a parallel to the suggestion that Othello charmed Desdemona away from her father by witchcraft. In Cinthio, the handkerchief is Moorish in style. Shakespeare changes this to Egyptian. Egypt was then believed, incorrectly, to be the home of the gypsies (hence their name), and gypsies were noted for charms and witchcraft. 'That handkerchief', Othello tells Desdemona,

> Did an Egyptian to my mother give:
> She was a charmer and could almost read
> The thoughts of people.   [III.iv.52–4]

If, in the late twentieth century we pay much attention to Brabantio's anger we probably think of it simply in terms of Desdemona running from the security of home to Othello's 'sooty bosom'. That is only a lesser reason for Brabantio's shock. At the time that the play was written, a man in his position would have been astonished at what his daughter had done and, even more, at the way Othello had behaved. Othello's superbly dignified response to the senators, and Desdemona's cool forensic power should not wholly persuade us otherwise. Shakespeare does not forget to mention the outcome: to Brabantio the 'match was mortal ... pure grief / Shore his old thread in twain' [v.ii.204–5]. It also lays Desdemona open to Iago's reminder to Othello, 'She did deceive her father' [III.iii.208], a warning Brabantio had uttered in the third scene: 'Look to her, Moor, if thou hast eyes to see: / She has deceived her father and may thee' [I.iii.288–9]. There can be little doubt that not a few in Jacobean England would have nodded approval. Thus are found together in Desdemona a spirited independence and a certain wilful irresponsibility.

Desdemona, in the tradition of nineteenth-century genteelness, can be seen as too innocent, too good to be true. If that does not quite accord with her independence of spirit, it accords even less with her sexuality. It is not unreasonable to suggest that if Desdemona was so ready to run from home into her beloved's bed that she must – like Othello – have been a passionate creature, though both could present a cool exterior. It is not easy to disentangle Iago's insinuations from fact. When he says to Roderigo, 'Didst thou not see her paddle with the palm of his hand? Didst not mark that?' [II.i.240], he might be creating an incident to sow a seed in Roderigo's mind or he may be lewdly describing natural lovingness. She can, perhaps, be best described as having a strong natural sexuality; there is little doubt that she is sexually attractive to Cassio, Roderigo, Iago and Othello. It is also evident that her independent nature enables her to relate freely and easily with men. Othello has a revealing line or two when he is trying to damp down his feelings of jealousy:

> To say my wife is fair, feeds well, loves company,
> Is free of speech, sings, plays, and dances well:
> Where virtue is, these are more virtuous.
> [III.iii.186–8]

These are, even Othello admits, innocent pleasures if the person engaging in them is virtuous. We know, and Othello learns too late, that his wife is virtuous, so her pleasures *are* innocent and they reveal Desdemona as being, quite as much as Othello, of 'a free and open nature' [I.iii.399]. I cannot help having in mind another dramatic picture of virtuous delight in the opposite sex: Shaw's Eliza Doolittle. Towards the end of *Pygmalion* she says to her mentor, Henry Higgins, 'I come – came – to care for you; not to want you to make love to me, and not forgetting the difference between us, but more friendly like.' Desdemona's free, open nature *is* sensual – as it has every right to be. Her tragedy is that, although her sexuality is directed solely towards Othello, other men, including (in the end, tragically) Othello, cannot comprehend her desire simply to be 'friendly like'. In such a society, a woman wishing only friendly, open relations with men could be taken by men to be sexually loose. If initially she allowed her independence to betray her into inconsiderateness, and so perhaps to give an impression to others that she might as readily desert Othello, she pays a heavy price for a small error of judgement. It is no more than that.

Contrasting characteristics are to be found in Othello to an
even more marked degree, and, whereas in the others they are
more or less held in balance, in Othello the tension between
them becomes too fierce; his nature is warped and his mind
breaks. The point about which this change turns is iv.i: the
trance or epileptic fit. Here the torment is so great that the
psychological stress takes physical form and Othello collapses.
What happens deserves detailed consideration, especially as it
brings together historic and dramatic convention, the language
of the play, and stage history.

Othello first appears to us, as is often pointed out by critics
and always performed, as calm and judicious (see his first line,
''Tis better as it is' [i.ii.6], and the speech that follows: 'Let him
do his spite: / My services which I have done the signiory /
Shall out-tongue his complaints'). He is perfectly self-assured
without being boastful. He can refer to his worth in a natural
manner – his descent from 'men of royal siege' and the services
he has done Venice. Looking back we may wonder whether he
is not too self-assured and so guilty of the sin of false security,
but we cannot know that when Othello first comes before us.
Later in that scene he exercises easy authority ('Keep up your
bright swords') and can ironically comment on the worth of
those wielding them – the dew is as like to rust them for lack of
proper use [59]. In the next scene, though I think we should not
gloss over his error in taking Desdemona without reference to
her father – surely in an Elizabethan or Jacobean context a
serious error – he shows poise and dignity as he twice addresses
the senators and explains how this has come about. Like
Desdemona, in an Elizabethan context, Othello is in the wrong
but the error is not such as to merit the tragic outcome: but that,
of course, is of the nature of tragedy. In performance it is
possible for the assembled senators to give some indication of
their sympathy for Brabantio's distress and their unease at
what Othello has done. This should be highlighted for a
modern audience so that it can better grasp what is at issue and
the tensions it prompts. The little exchange when Brabantio
enters is worth noting. The Duke is all eyes for Othello, the man
for the moment; he does not even notice Brabantio. When he
does he says, 'We lacked your counsel and your help tonight',
and Brabantio sharply replies, accurately forecasting what will
happen, 'So did I yours.' But Othello is needed by Venice as its

commander agains the Turks, and a political decision must be made in which the state takes precedence over the individual. The Duke's easy platitudes [197–207] are seen by Brabantio for just what they are, a politician's glib truisms: 'He bears the sentence well that nothing bears' [210]. Desdemona and Othello even persuade the Duke to permit her to accompany her husband to Cyprus, there to be provided with 'such accommodation and besort / As levels with her breeding' [235–6], despite Brabantio's sharp denial of their request. In the architecture of the play, Brabantio's cry for a lost daughter anticipates Othello's for a wife lost to him.

After the arrival in Cyprus, Iago works upon Othello and his perplexity increases. Up until Act IV his language, though beginning to show a lack of control and an absence of that calm, dignified poise of the first act, is never seriously immoderate, although at the end of III.iii there is a hint of what is to come as he thinks of killing his wife: 'Damn her, lewd minx! O, damn her, damn her!' [476]. At IV.i, however, there is a shattering change in Othello's demeanour. We have just witnessed the confrontation in which, most injudiciously, Desdemona appeals on Cassio's behalf only to have her requests punctuated by Othello's jealous demands for the handkerchief. As Iago and Othello enter at the beginning of the fourth act, Iago is poisoning Othello's mind, taunting him with the physical details of a sexual encounter – from kissing to lying naked in bed with Cassio 'An hour or more, and not mean harm?' [IV.i.5]. Thirty lines later, Iago slips the word 'Lie' into Othello's mind again. Othello becomes distraught. His mind hovers over the sexual implications of 'lie' and his language breaks up like some tragic Mr Jingle – 'Handkerchief – confessions – handkerchief' and, then, 'Pish! Noses, ears, and lips. Is't possible? – Confess? Handkerchief? O devil!'. He then falls into a trance. The final cry, 'O devil!' presumably refers to Desdemona, but suggests also the devil that has taken control of him.

Othello's fit is representative of more than the physical expression of his mental torment. It has been suggested (by Lawrence J. Ross) that, in Othello's prostration, Shakespeare is utilising a morality-play convention in which the once-virtuous fall beneath the foot of the devil. It is the reverse of the figure of Virtue triumphing over Vice. On the page, this disposition of the characters can almost pass unnoticed; in the theatre it should impress our imaginations strongly, and that can be enhanced by the stage business which Granville-Barker mentions (and Ross notes): 'Actors of Iago are accustomed to put their foot, for a moment, upon the prostrate body, even to give it a slight, contemptuous kick. This is wholly appropriate' (1963, p. 193). Othello is not alone of Shakespeare's characters in suffering such a fit. Julius Caesar (historically and in Shakespeare's play) suffered from 'falling-sickness'. But in Caesar this was a condition natural to him. Despite Iago's telling Cassio a few lines later that this is Othello's second fit (quite probably a lie), it is not natural to Othello but has quite suddenly been brought upon him. Further, it is an invention of Shakespeare's – it does not occur in Cinthio's story. In Shakespeare's time, Othello's epileptic fit, prompted as it is by that 'O devil!', must appear to be a form of demonic possession. Hobbes, in *Leviathan* (1651), III, 34, 211, speaks of epileptics being considered demoniacs, i.e. possessed by devils. That may be lost on a modern audience, but Elizabethans would surely think of instances of possession and the casting-out of devils in the New Testament (e.g. Matthew 4:24 and Luke 11:20). To a modern audience it will simply seem that the antithetical forces characterising Othello are no longer in balance; the tensions have proved too strong and Othello's psychological disintegration has taken physical form, but the Elizabethan 'dimension' is important to a full understanding and enactment of the play. John Vyvyan also recognises demonic possession in Othello but places it earlier. At III.iii.477ff. Othello suggests to Iago,

> Come, go with me apart. I will withdraw
> To furnish me with some swift means of death
> For the fair devil.

Then, very significantly, he tells Iago, 'Now art thou my lieutenant', to which Iago responds, 'I am your own for ever' – and the scene ends (Vyvyan, 1959, p. 103). This, surely, is much more than a mere replacement for the disgraced Cassio. It reeks more of the relationship between Doctor Faustus and Mephostophilis.

It is not easy to get across to a modern audience the full force of what has happened to Othello, even though in his language the diabolic imagery has passed from Iago to him. What is plain when he recovers is how his language has deteriorated into a violent lewdness which matches that of Iago in the first scene – 'an old black ram / Is tupping your white ewe' [i.i.89–90], 'your daughter covered with a Barbary horse' [111], and 'making the beast with two backs' [116]. All that was so loathsome in Iago is now found in Othello. In iv.ii he treats Emilia as 'a simple bawd' to her mistress, 'a subtle whore' [19, 20], and behaves as if he were in a brothel. This is ironically reinforced by Desdemona's innocent questions when she enters: 'My lord, what is your will?' and 'What is your pleasure?' – questions a prostitute might ask a customer. Othello then sends Emilia away to stand guard:

> Some of your function [as bawd], mistress:
> Leave procreants alone and shut the door;
> Cough or cry 'hem' if anybody come.
> Your mystery, your mystery [your trade as bawd]!
> [26–9]

His images of 'foul toads' who 'knot and gender' [60–1], of 'summer flies in the shambles, / That quicken even with blowing' [65–6], his description of Desdemona as a weed [66], and the way he directly calls her 'whore' [85 and 89] and tells her that she, like a prostitute, keeps the gates of hell [91], prior to offering her money [92], indicate just how deranged he has become and how vividly Shakespeare portrays the way Othello has been 'possessed' by Iago's vile, devil, nature.

When Desdemona innocently asks what sin she has committed [69], Othello begins by heaping further insults upon her and then involves all nature in his assault. 'Committed' is made to imply adultery, a 'commoner' here means a prostitute, and he also calls her 'strumpet'. But heaven 'stopping the nose' and the chaste moon winking suggest they both condone her supposed sexual misdemeanours, and the wind (by a device known as 'pathetic fallacy', by which natural elements are given human characteristics) is said to be bawdy, its movement over the earth being described as 'kissing' – here not a gentle touching of one natural object against another as it brushes past but a lascivious embrace. The 'accusations' levelled at nature are patently absurd, as groundless as those with which Othello charges Desdemona. The speech indicates her innocence and the degree to which Othello's distress has deranged his judgement.

Between the scene of Othello's fit and his treating Desdemona and Emilia as prostitute and bawd comes an interlude of black farce. In Part One of this study some attention was paid to the comedic structure of *Othello* and certain other characteristics of comedy. The scene in which Iago and Cassio discuss Bianca, and Othello is placed so that he can overhear them, but, fatally, only overhear misleadingly, is typical of comedy. Here the device straddles a razor's edge between the comic and the pathetic. It dramatises from a different perspective Othello's imbalance, the depths to which he has sunk from the dignified commander of the play's opening. For the audience, the bitter humour and pain are held in tension, tightening the play's grip on the imagination and transferring some of Othello's anguish to those witnessing – participators in – the performance.

Iago's success does not end with his domination of Othello, graphically represented for us by his standing atop his fallen commander. After Othello has left Desdemona she shares her distress with Emilia. When Iago enters, Emilia explains that Othello has 'so bewhored her' and spoken so despitefully to her that it is more than true hearts can bear. Desdemona cannot bring herself to say the word 'whore' in asking Iago whether she is 'that name', and it is noticeable that Iago doesn't use the word either. His attitude is very much as if the whole thing is no more than a storm in a teacup brought on by the pressure of affairs of state. But the scene has two conflicting elements that continue the 'razor's-edge technique' and make it a parallel to Iago's triumph over Othello. Emilia, who would not be out of place in a comedy, speaks unwittingly of her husband as 'some external villain, / Some busy and insinuating rogue, / Some cogging cozening slave' who has devised this slander [IV.ii.129–31]. She continues in the same strain with such vehemence that Iago feels constrained to tell her to keep her voice down. Now, Emilia's speech in another context, delivered unawares before the guilty person, would be comic. But she also touches on the nub of what is at bottom of this 'device': 'some external villain' – Iago as devil. That is an appropriate reminder, were any needed, when Desdemona, only too ready to pardon such a villain [135], appeals to Iago *on her knees* [150]. What she then offers is, in effect, a confessional prayer, appropriate in church, horribly incongruous made as if to Iago. Iago's triumph is complete and it is again presented by Shakespeare in pictorial as well as verbal terms.

One tiny touch in that speech is worth comment. Earlier in the scene Desdemona has not been able to bring herself to say 'whore'. At l.160 she says, 'I cannot say "whore"'. Again, the effect in another context could be comic. (It was a commonplace music-hall device – 'I cannot', the fool would explain, 'say ari-ari-ari-arithmetic', and then never stop assuring us he couldn't say the word.) Obviously it is not comic here, but there is just a hint of paradox to which the actress will draw attention by the reluctance with which she utters this sentence. The technique is deeply touching. Shaw, in that little extract quoted earlier, uses a similar technique when he has Eliza stumble over her grammar – 'come'/'came'. This catches at the heartstrings, and in a single word all that has past, for good or ill for Eliza or Desdemona, is conjured up before us.

Othello's final speech and action have attracted adverse criticism. Quite how so fine a poet and critic as T. S. Eliot could reduce this to Othello cheering himself up is puzzling. It is very much a case of Homer nodding. But some attacks have been more sustained, as have defences of Othello (and these have been touched on in Part One). Instead of being viewed as melodramatic self-dramatisation, this moment is better seen in the context of the pattern of the whole play (and Maynard Mack's outline of the overall movement in Jacobean tragedies is helpful). The speech is parallel to those Othello addresses to the Senate. All three are designed to justify his actions (and I shall return in a moment to one action that needs justification). A tragic hero in a poetic drama inevitably expresses himself at such crucial moments in particularly 'poetic', self-revealing language. That doesn't make Othello guilty of self-dramatisation any more than Richard II fails as a king because he is really a poet (though that argument has been advanced). Othello, in fact, is far less prone to self-dramatisation than is Richard in his final soliloquy in his cell. In the course of the speech Othello, aware of the good service he has done the state, sees how little it counts for in comparison to what he has done through perplexity, not malice; recognises how precious was the pearl he so carelessly tossed away; recovers something of his former dignity now that his mind has cleared; likens himself to 'a malignant . . . Turk' who 'Beat a Venetian and traduced the state' (actions Othello implies he has now done); and then finally consigns himself to eternal perdition. For this is suicide (as Othello himself says, 'Killing myself, to die upon a kiss'), and, in the Christian framework within which the play is set and was first received, that was the fate of those who took their own lives. There is thus no question, as for Hamlet, of flights of angels winging Othello to eternal rest. The mood of the ending is far closer to that of *King Lear*. We are a world away from Othello 'cheering himself up' or finding easy comfort.

Othello and tragic error

The tragic hero's downfall, said Aristotle in the *Poetics*, was brought upon him not by vice and depravity but by some error of judgement. Aristotle's theory is not the final word on tragedy but, rightly read, it can be helpful, and as it happens, can usefully point to what is going on in *Othello*. This tragic 'flaw' (*hamartia*) has sometimes been incorrectly interpreted in moral terms, and some critics (and many more students) have looked for some moral weakness in the tragic hero. For *Othello*, this has led to the commonplace assertion that Othello falls because he was too jealous – hence the arguments about whether he was naturally or racially prone to jealousy, or easily made jealous, and so on. But this is to miss Aristotle's point. Obviously Othello becomes jealous, but we can productively short-circuit the argument about whether he was naturally jealous or not by looking for 'error of judgement' rather than moral flaw.

Othello's downfall may be said to be a result of racial prejudice. That might accord with current responses and would not be inappropriate in Shakespeare's time, but Othello's colour can hardly be said to be an error of judgement on his part. I don't think his fall was prompted by colour or racial attitudes though there can be little doubt that both intensify the conflict for him and for us. Othello does make two plain errors of judgement and Desdemona shares in both. Implicit trust is placed in Iago and there can be no denying that

Iago is the agent for their fall. But he is not the prime cause. As Marlowe shows very clearly in *Doctor Faustus*, Mephostophilis can only operate if his victim has himself prepared the ground and the hero has laid himself open to temptation. Iago's insinuations would not work were there no fertile ground. The error of judgement that Othello and Desdemona jointly make can be traced back to the manner of their marriage. We, humanely and rather romantically – 'All the world loves a lover' – gloss over what they have done. It was no great wickedness for Othello to take Desdemona off to be married in secret without her father's consent, or for her to go, willingly, or for them to take lodging in the Sagittary. There is no 'moral flaw'. But it was pretty stupid. It was an action that might well be forgiven in a young girl, but it was hardly the intelligent or considerate behaviour of someone of Othello's age and experience. At that time, such behaviour was reprehensible – which doesn't mean it never happened. But, as in the secret marriage of the Duchess of Malfi, whose actions strike a modern audience as unexceptionable, great offence has been given to the accepted canons of the day. A serious error of judgement has been made, and it is not difficult, when one looks, to read between the lines when Brabantio, Othello and Desdemona appear before the senators and realise that the couple's behaviour was irregular. On the stage it needs to be made more apparent.

All else is set in train by their error of judgement. Othello and Desdemona are laid open to the abuse and sexual innuendo of Iago; the discrepancy between age and youth is pointed to; the differences in nationality, colour and race become an issue which can be twisted this way and that by the malicious; Desdemona's deception of her father (for that is what it is) not only leads to his death but can later be used against her – she deceived her father and may deceive you, Othello; the different values of a soldier's life and that of a Venetian can be exposed.

To pick up Arthur Miller again – *Othello* isn't 'about' jealousy, or race, or even prejudice broadly interpreted. It most certainly isn't about deceiving a father and marrying in secret. One virtue of tracing the error to this event is that it knocks on the head many attempts to fix what the play is said to be about. No one would argue the play is 'about' such an error. First and foremost the play is, in Miller's terms, 'about itself': it is its own world. We may draw parallels with the world we know; we can certainly recognise similarities even if our world and Shakespeare's differ in detail. That is why the play still speaks to us so 'dramatically'. But we need to see how the action of the play springs from within it rather than attempt to import into it our moral concerns.

Double time and its implications

If the principal characters are created of conflicting characteristics, much the same might be said of the structure of *Othello*. Ned B. Allen has examined in detail in 'The Two Parts of *Othello*' the process of composition by which the double-time scheme became established in *Othello*. His suppositions are convincing, as are his descriptions of certain characteristics of the play in relation to this pattern of double-time. Thus, he notes that the first two acts and III.i are related only lightly to the source, Cinthio, but thereafter the source is much more closely followed and there are a number of verbal similarities. And there are contradictions. The action can be taken to follow straight through, but there is also an assumption in Act III that Othello and Desdemona have been married for several weeks or even months. Perhaps more significant in performance, Professor Allen also points to the even course of action of the first two acts; these progress as in our everyday lives. However, the last three acts move with 'horrifying speed'. Thus, double time is 'one of the contrasting features of the two parts of *Othello*' (*ShS 21*, pp. 15, 16). Having worked out how this may have arisen, Professor Allen suggests that Shakespeare spliced two parts of *Othello* written at different times and 'not originally intended to go together'. That hypothesis he finds more acceptable that one supposing that the play as we have it 'was born whole but imperfectly formed in his mind'; economy might explain the first (preferred) hypothesis, but the second 'can have no satisfactory explanation' (p. 25). Whether or not one agrees with Professor Allen's conclusions, he gives many illuminating insights into the structure of *Othello*.

Many people consider this matter of double time an academic irrelevance. To L. C. Knights it was one of 'the vagaries that serve as Shakespeare criticism' arising from the

'habit of regarding Shakespeare's persons as "friends for life"
or, maybe, "deceased acquaintances"' (1964, p. 27). It is
frequently pointed out that though it 'has so vexed critics . . . it
does not trouble spectators'. It is, continues Dame Helen
Gardner, in accord with the 'conception of love as beyond
nature. That lovers' time is not the time of the seasons is a
commonplace' (C, p. 154). A special theory of relativity might
apply in physics and in comedy – it certainly is skilfully and
amusingly deployed in *As You Like It* – but, applied like this to
Othello as an invitation to us to ignore the possible relevance of
the patterns of time, it sounds like special pleading, as are some
of the exculpations offered. Certainly, some critics 'resent the
way that Shakespeare hypnotizes us into believing
impossibilities', as Kenneth Muir describes the responses of
Stoll and Robert Bridges (1978, p. 194). It must be admitted
that for some people the lack of opportunity for adultery to have
been committed by Cassio and Desdemona is a stumbling-
block; in a modern play *in the realistic tradition* it would prove a
very serious flaw.

W. H. Auden seems to me nearer the mark:

> Some critics have taken the double time in the play to be
> merely a dramaturgical device for speeding the action which
> the audience in the theatre will never notice. I believe,
> however, that Shakespeare meant the audience to notice it
> as, in *The Merchant of Venice*, he meant them to notice the
> discrepancy between Belmont time and Venice time.

The reason he gives deserves consideration:

> Othello is not merely jealous of feelings which might exist; he
> demands proof of an act which could not have taken place,
> and the effect on him of believing in this physical
> impossibility goes far beyond wishing to kill her: it is not only
> his wife who has betrayed him but the whole universe; life
> has become meaningless, his occupation is gone. (C,
> p. 216)

May there not be more to double time than careless
carpentering of chips from the workshop, or, even, Muir's fairer
assessment of Shakespeare's joinery: 'sheer technical mastery'

(1978, p. 194)? Might it not be proper to consider this as a double-time *scheme*? If the audience notice that 'the time is out of joint' in *Othello*, they will stand slightly distanced from the action, act as witnesses to a tragedy, as it were; if they fail to notice (or to regard this as important in scholarly discussions), then they act as participants. And here the comedic structure so many critics have seen underlying *Othello* also comes into play. There is an element of detachment in witnessing comedy and a characteristic involvement for an audience of tragedy. Consider the razor's edge of attitudes and emotions involved (as indicated above) in witnessing Othello overhearing Iago and Desdemona laughing about Bianca in iv.i and hearing Desdemona say, 'I cannot say "whore"' [iv.ii.160]. Might it not be that a reason for the undoubted tension we feel in witnessing *Othello* derives from the way we are caught between responses, between witnessing and participating? The conflicts within characters extend not only to the time scheme of the play, but to its roots in the two opposed forms, tragedy and comedy, and thence to the audience.

In discussing the historical-critical approach no mention was made of one shift in our mode of apprehension that is of great importance when considering drama written prior to about 1850: attitudes to realism. With the advent of realism in literature, and especially in drama, the photograph and the opportunities it gave for pictorial journalism, the cinema and the newsreel camera, and finally television, it has come about that throughout our lives we are constantly being presented with images of things as they are – or, at least, as they are purported to be. Thus Chekhov in 1887: 'Artistic literature is called so just because it depicts life as it really is. . . . A writer must be as objective as a chemist . . . he must know that dung-heaps play a very respectable part in a landscape, and that evil passions are as inherent in life as good ones' [Ellmann and Feidelson, 1965, p. 245]. This is not to say that Shakespeare was not concerned with 'life as it really is', but rather to say that in his day the way in which drama represented life was different. No one can doubt that Shakespeare in *Othello*, and specifically in Iago, dramatises inherent evil passions, but we may be in danger, because we see Shakespeare through a veil of realistic expectation, of demanding that he conform to concepts of realistic art quite foreign to him and every other pre-nineteenth-century writer.

Let us imagine that Shakespeare *did* cobble up two disparate parts of plays. Is it seriously argued that he was so imperceptive as not to notice that the times were awry? Or is it suggested he was so poor a craftsman that he couldn't manipulate the time scheme so that it could be consistent? And, even if the answers to both questions are 'yes', would not his fellow actors have pointed out the error, if that is what it was? It *is* conceivable that in the course of writing *Othello*, and perhaps even joining together two parts, Shakespeare found that the time patterns failed to chime well together. But might he not have realised, as even the most ordinary writers have done, that out of some fortuitous accident some dramatic point might be made? If not designed from the start, double time in *Othello* may well be an artistically productive accident. It is worth contrasting inconsistencies or illogicalities that are to be found in a couple of other plays.

Lewis Carroll, as author of *Alice in Wonderland* a writer with some acquaintance with seeming inconsistency for artistic ends, wrote to the actress Ellen Terry and pointed out that in *Much Ado about Nothing* Hero or Beatrice should have been easily able to produce an alibi demonstrating that Claudio's accusation was groundless. This may be an oversight by Shakespeare. I've never taught a student who has noticed this slip unprompted and it is perhaps the kind of error that could have gone unnoticed by Shakespeare and his fellows. It is simply not possible to equate the double time with Hero's missing alibi.

The improbabilities of *King Lear* are another matter and in dramatic mood bring us closer to *Othello* than does *Much Ado about Nothing*. L. C. Knights remarked in '*King Lear* as Metaphor',

> in *King Lear*, Shakespeare is far from concerning himself with naturalistic illusion. Not only are there bold improbabilities (the parallel plots, Edgar's disguises, Dover cliff, etc.), there is an almost complete rejection of verisimilitude in the portrayal of the characters and their setting, of anything that might seem to keep us in close touch with a familiar – or at all events an actual – world.   (1963, p. 27)

Othello has a lesser variety of 'improbabilities', but it is not unreasonable to suggest that the 'non-realistic' element of this play is a characteristic developed further by Shakespeare in *King Lear*. A little later in his essay Professor Knights says, 'The questions raised by *King Lear* do not allow "explanations" that you can complacently store in a pocket of the mind: they seemed designed to cause the greatest possible uncertainty, or even bewilderment' (p. 30).

King Lear fractures reality in a more thoroughgoing manner than does *Othello*, so our sense of bewilderment at the improbability of double time is not so extreme. Indeed, the uncertainty is, perhaps, not marked enough, so that, as in *Much Ado about Nothing*, we may overlook – even be invited by critics – to overlook this inconsistency. It is, however, an integral part of the design, I believe. Kenneth Muir commented on the double time of the play, 'There is certainly a deliberate confusion of the time-scheme' (1978, p. 194). It is intended to cause us a degree of uncertainty so that in our responses we may not fall back on our comfortable certainties – in effect, our prejudices.

An aspect of *Othello* that is not in dispute might now usefully be touched on. It is noticeable how many characters are deceived in the play, and how very easily. It is a commonplace of rather unthinking criticism to pin the whole play down to confusion over a lost handkerchief. As Rymer pungently puts it, 'Had it been *Desdemona's* Garter, the Sagacious Moor might have smelt a Rat; but the Handerkerchief is so remote a trifle, no Booby on this side *Mauretania* cou'd make any consequence from it' (*C*, p. 44). But the handkerchief device is but a small, though to us prominent, element in a web of deception. Roderigo, Emilia and Cassio, as well as Desdemona and Othello, are deceived by Iago in ways important to the plot. Even so minor a character as Lodovico is deceived. He considers Iago 'a very valiant fellow' at v.i.52 and earlier he accepts Iago at face value yet can tell Iago he is sorry that he has been deceived in Othello [iv.i.273].

We too may be deceived by Iago, even against our better judgement, but, we may also be deceived into assuming because we are unfamiliar with Elizabethan conventions, the marriage of Othello and Desdemona is a romantic elopement and so letting it pass us by without comment. It is curious, too, how many of the play's ironies and inversions can pass unnoticed. Iago's protestations of his honesty we can see through, at least in a general sense. It is ironical that Cassio, said by Iago to be an inexperienced Florentine arithmetician, 'almost damned in a fair wife, / That never set a squadron in the field . . . a bookish theoric' [i.i.19–24], easily made drunk, replaces Othello as Governor. The irony that honest Iago is innately jealous and jealous Othello implicity trustful has been pointed to, as has the contrast between black-visaged Othello and black-hearted Iago. These kinds of irony and inversion are pervasive and to be found in even passing incidents and lines. Thus, Othello assures the senators that taking his wife with him will not interfere with his duties: 'heaven defend your good souls that you think / I will your great business scant / For she is with me' [i.iii.262–4]. It is a mark of the Duke's unease (which again probably passes us by) that his only decision is to leave it to Othello's private determination – 'Th'affair cries haste, / And speed must answer it' [i.iii.271–3]. Short-sighted political expediency gives the answer and, as it turns out, domestic strife, murder and suicide follow. Finally, brief mention may be made of two of many instances that could be given to illustrate the rich irony of the dialogue. First, at i.iii.290 Othello swears, 'My life upon her faith': his death (and hers) follow on Othello's *lack* of faith. Secondly, Iago comforts Desdemona and Emilia at iv.ii.170 with, 'Go in and weep not; all things shall be well.' They will, of course, be far from well, as Iago knows. The assurance of this old Anglo-Saxon formula is hollow.

Shakespeare dramatises in *Othello* a story of wondrous love, of a relationship many find hard to accept, whether they are characters in the play-world or members of the audience. He embeds this story in an intricate web of ironies, inversions, and deceptions, not least of which is what we may now boldly call his double-time-scheme. Time after time our capacity to make true judgements, consciously or subconsciously, is probed. In the old morality plays (with which we know Shakespeare was familiar, referring to them directly and drawing upon them – for Falstaff, for example), the Vice tempted the audience. So, in this play, not only does the Devil/Vice Iago attempt to seduce us into seeing things his way, but the structural design can trick our expectations and confuse our power to judge. Perhaps the greatest irony of all is that it is the world of wonder, the love story of a young Venetian girl and a black commander of royal descent, coming to us, as Bradley justly put it, from a wonderland (*C*, p. 57), that gives the reality that we should accept, and that it is all the machinations of the 'real' world that we should test and, frequently, find wanting. Shakespeare's genius and his sheer craftsmanship must make us take his apparent inconsistencies seriously and see where they lead us. No one can doubt the masterly dramatic art of the Dover cliff scene in *King Lear*, yet it is as 'impossible' as any moment in Shakespeare's plays. Shakespeare's time scheme in *Othello* is one means whereby we can see through into the art and the truth of this play that, in the theatre, justly moves audiences so deeply.

Further Reading and References

OF BOOK-LENGTH studies offering detailed accounts of
Othello, three might be found especially helpful. Robert B.
Heilman's *Magic in the Web* (1956) is concerned, as its sub-title
suggests, with 'action and language'. It pays particular
attention to Iago and Othello (more to the former than the
latter). It has a well-arranged index that enables the reader to
find easily what Heilman has to say about, say, Othello 'as
man of reason', or Iago and Desdemona 'as element in
Othello', or all three 'as physician'. Themes (such as 'light and
dark') and imagery are indexed.

Marvin Rosenberg's *The Masks of Othello* (1961) is well
described by its sub-title: 'The Search for the Identity of
Othello, Iago, and Desdemona by Three Centuries of Actors
and Critics'. This is just, up to a point, but the result is not *quite*
so theatre-oriented as might be expected. The reader might feel
that the search has been pre-empted by Rosenberg's having,
from his point of view, successfully completed the search for
himself in advance. The study of what actors have done is
conditioned by Rosenberg's concept of 'the identity' that will
(for him) best work in the theatre. The book is nevertheless
valuable but less open than it might be.

A more recent study is Jane Adamson's *'Othello' as Tragedy:
Some Problems of Judgment and Feeling* (1980), the limitations of
which (set by the author herself) have been mentioned earlier.
Dr Adamson endeavours 'to turn back to the play again and ask
why has it proved so hard for critics to reach even a rough
general agreement about its basic tenor, about what we make of
its hero, and about the kind, depth and scope of the demands it
makes on us' (p. 2). *Othello*, she argues, 'dramatizes and
explores the ways and means by which different people "make
sense" of what happens in their lives, including what they

merely imagine to be happening . . . how every one of the characters construes and misconstrues things, how they all "fashion" their view of others to fit with their sense of themselves (or vice versa)' (pp. 2–3). This study offers a fresh appraisal of *Othello* and often in a usefully different way from that given here.

The advantage of a volume wholly devoted to one play is obvious. It can make a thorough analysis, even line-by-line, as G. R. Elliott does in *Flaming Minister: A Study of 'Othello' as Tragedy of Love and Hate* (1953). The disadvantage is well put by Robert Heilman – it is one man's (or woman's) reading.

Two studies which have attained classic status should not be passed over. A. C. Bradley's two lectures on *Othello* in *Shakespearean Tragedy* (1904; 2nd edn 1905; readily available in paperback) have stood the test of time amazingly well, despite – perhaps because of – attacks made upon them and him. If the animosity is ignored, the criticisms of Bradley's view can be a useful corrective. Bradley's criticism of *Othello* also has two unusual virtues. When he slips up it is fairly obvious, so that a modern reader is not likely to be misled; and, after nearly a century, his enthusiasm still communicates itself to the reader and that is unusual in criticism. Bradley should be read in full and not solely in the brief extract reproduced in the Macmillan *Casebook*.

Harley Granville-Barker's Preface to *Othello* (in vol. 4 of his collected *Prefaces*) is a rather discursive account but it is full of useful insights and informed by the combined experience of a great man of the theatre and a perceptive critic. The Prefaces date back over half a century; the illustrated paperback edition published by Batsford (1963), with notes by M. St. Clare Byrne, should be sought. Another form of 'illustration' that can be readily studied is the video of Olivier's film of *Othello*. This can be hired cheaply.

Two general studies are recommended: Emrys Jones's *Scenic Form in Shakespeare* (1971) and John Vyvyan's *The Shakespeare Ethic* (1959). The former has an excellent chapter on *Othello* (pp. 117–51) and is also more broadly useful in its analysis of scenic construction and relating the construction of one play to that of another. Vyvyan has a short but perceptive chapter on *Othello* (pp. 95–103) and this is to be read in the context of his general aim. 'Shakespeare's tragic characters', he says, 'are continually asking themselves questions . . . What ought I to do?', but, 'In the opinion of some critics . . . for us to ask such a question is illegitimate' (p. 9). He explores Shakespeare's 'increasing fascination' with the ethical problems posed by the plays (p. 11). He is particularly good on what he calls the 'allegorical composition' of the plays (p. 101).

Two volumes of essays often referred to in this study are mainly or entirely devoted to *Othello*. The Macmillan *Casebook* on the play (1971) has a lengthy introduction by the editor, John Wain, brief extracts from Samuel Johnson and Samuel Taylor Coleridge, and a generous slab of Thomas Rymer's *A Short View of Tragedy* (1693). There is a fragment from the first of Bradley's lectures on *Othello*; a relevant page or two from T. S. Eliot's 'Shakespeare and the Stoicism of Seneca' (1927), which is the source of the remark that in his last speech Othello is 'cheering himself up'; and the following in full or in generous extracts.

G. Wilson Knight, 'The *Othello* Music', from *The Wheel of Fire* (1930).
William Empson, 'Honest in *Othello*', from *The Structure of Complex Words* (1951).
F. R. Leavis, 'Diabolic Intellect and the Noble Hero', from *The Common Pursuit* (1952).
Helen Gardner, 'The Noble Moor', *Proceedings of the British Academy*, 41 (1956).
John Bayley, 'Love and Identity: *Othello*', from *The Characters of Love* (1962).
W. H. Auden, 'The Joker in the Pack', from *The Dyer's Hand* (1963).
Nevill Coghill, extracts from *Shakespeare's Professional Skills* (1964).

The second volume is *Shakespeare Survey 21*, ed. Kenneth Muir (1970). This has nine excellent articles. Three are on Othello as seen by Rymer, Delacroix and Verdi; the others (all referred to above) are as follows.

Helen Gardner, '*Othello*: A Retrospect, 1900–67'.
Ned B. Allen, 'The Two Parts of *Othello*'.

B. H. C. de Mendonça, '*Othello*: A Tragedy Built on a Comic Structure'.
G. R. Hibbard, '*Othello* and the Patterns of Shakespearian Tragedy'.
Emrys Jones, '*Othello*, Lepanto and the Cyprus Wars'.
Leah Scragg, 'Iago – Vice or Devil?'

One more article should certainly be dug out: G. K. Hunter's 'Othello and Colour Prejudice' (1967, repr. 1978).
The following list includes all sources cited in the text by author and date, plus some other helpful studies.

Adamson, Jane, '*Othello' as Tragedy: Some Problems of Judgment and Feeling* (Cambridge, 1980).
Barthes, Roland, 'Myth Today', *Mythologies* (London 1972; paperback edn 1973).
Battenhouse, Roy W., 'Shakespearean Tragedy: A Christian Approach', in *Approaches to Shakespeare*, ed. N. Rabkin (New York, 1964), pp. 203–16.
Bodkin, Maud, *Archetypal Patterns in Poetry: Psychological Studies of Imagination* (Oxford, 1934).
Bradley, A. C., *Shakespearean Tragedy* (London, 1904; 2nd edn 1905).
Campbell, Lily B., *Shakespeare's Tragic Heroes: Slaves of Passion* (Cambridge, 1930).
Clemen, Wolfgang, *The Development of Shakespeare's Imagery* (London, 1951).
——, *Shakespeare's Soliloquies* (Cambridge, 1964).
Colman, E. A. M., '*Hamlet*: The Poem or the Play?', *Sydney Studies in English*, 1 (1975–6), pp. 3–12.
David, Richard, *Shakespeare in the Theatre* (Cambridge, 1978).
Dean, Leonard F. (ed.), *A Casebook on 'Othello'* (Binghampton, NY, 1961). Includes 13 items.
Draper, John W., *The Othello of Shakespeare's Audience* (New York, 1966).
Ellman, R., and Feidelson, C. (eds), *The Modern Tradition* (New York, 1965).
Elliot, G. R., *Flaming Minister: A Study of 'Othello' as Tragedy of Love and Hate* (Durham, NC, 1953).
Everett, Barbara, 'Reflections on the Sentimentalist's *Othello*', *Critical Quarterly*, 3 (1961).

Flatter, Richard, *The Moor of Venice* (London, 1950).

Foakes, R. A., 'Suggestions for a New Approach to Shakespeare's Imagery', *Shakespeare Survey* (Cambridge, 1952), pp. 81–92.

Frye, Northrop, *The Anatomy of Criticism* (Princeton, NJ, 1957).

——, 'The Road to Excess', in B. Slote (ed.), *Myth and Symbol* (Lincoln, Nebr., 1963), pp. 3–20.

Goddard, Harold, *The Meaning of Shakespeare*, 2 vols (Chicago, 1951).

Granville-Barker, Harley, *Prefaces*, with notes by M. St Clare Byrne (London, 1963).

Gribble, James, *Literary Education: A Revaluation* (Cambridge, 1983).

Harris, Bernard, 'A Portrait of a Moor', *Shakespeare Survey 11* (Cambridge, 1958), pp. 89–97. This includes a full-page reproduction of the portrait of the Moorish ambassador to Queen Elizabeth painted in 1600.

Harrison, G. B., *Shakespeare's Tragedies* (London, 1951).

Heilman, Robert B., *Magic in the Web* (Lexington, Ky, 1956).

Holloway, John, *The Story of the Night* (London, 1961); see pp. 37–56 and Appendix A, 'Dr Leavis and "Diabolic Intellect"', pp. 155–65.

Hunter, G. K., 'Othello and Colour Prejudice', *Proceedings of the British Academy*, 53 (1967); repr. in Hunter, *Dramatic Identities and Cultural Tradition* (Liverpool, 1978), pp. 31–59.

Jones, Eldred, *Othello's Countrymen: The African in English Renaissance Drama* (London, 1965).

Jones, Emrys, *Scenic Form in Shakespeare* (Oxford, 1971).

Kaula, David, 'Othello Possessed: Notes on Shakespeare's Use of Magic and Witchcraft', *Shakespeare Studies*, 1966, pp. 112–32.

Knights, L. C., 'How Many Children had Lady Macbeth' in *Explorations* (London, 1946; Harmondsworth, 1964).

——, '*King Lear* as Metaphor', in B. Slote (ed.), *Myth and Symbol* (Lincoln, Nebr., 1963), pp. 21–38.

——, 'The Question of Character in Shakespeare's Plays' (1959), repr. in his *Further Explorations* (London, 1965).

Lees, F. N., 'Othello's Name', *Notes and Queries*, n.s. 8 (1961) p. 139.

Lodge, David (ed.), *20th Century Literary Criticism: A Reader*

(London, 1972). Includes Susan Sontag's 'Against Interpretation'.

McAlindon, T., *Shakespeare and Decorum* (London, 1973).

Mack, Maynard, 'The Jacobean Shakespeare', *Jacobean Theatre*, Stratford-on-Avon Studies 1, ed. J. R. Brown and B. Harris (London, 1960).

Matthews, G. M., '*Othello* and the Dignity of Man', in Arnold Kettle (ed.), *Shakespeare in a Changing World* (London, 1964); repr. in David Craig (ed.), *Marxists on Literature* (Harmondsworth, 1975) pp. 110–33.

Morozov, Mikhail M., 'The Individualization of Shakespeare's Characters through Imagery', *Shakespeare Survey* 2 (Cambridge, 1949), pp. 83–106; pp. 84–90 are devoted to Othello, Iago and Desdemona.

Muir, Kenneth, *Shakespeare's Tragic Sequence* (London, 1972).

——, *The Sources of Shakespeare's Plays* (New Haven, Conn., 1978).

—— (ed.), *Shakespeare Survey 21* (Cambridge, 1970). See details on p. 88–9.

Miller, Arthur, *The Theater Essays of Arthur Miller*, ed. R. A. Martin (Harmondsworth, 1978).

Rosenburg, Marvin, *The Masks of Othello* (Berkeley, Calif., 1961).

Ross, Lawrence J. (ed.), *Othello* (Indianapolis, 1974).

Samarin, R., and Nikolyukin, A. (eds), *Shakespeare in the Soviet Union*, tr. A. Pyman (Moscow, 1966).

Sanders, Norman (ed.), *Othello*, New Cambridge edn (Cambridge, 1984).

Schlegel, A. W., *A Course of Lectures on Dramatic Art and Literature*, 2 vols, tr. John Black, 2nd edn (London, 1840).

Scott, Wilbur (ed.), *Five Approaches of Literary Criticism* (New York, 1962, 1972). Includes extract from Leslie Fiedler, *An End of Innocence* (1952), together with useful introductions to literary critical approaches and good illustrative essays.

Sontag, Susan, 'Against Interpretation' (1964), repr. in her *Against Interpretation and Other Essays* (New York, 1969), and in Lodge (1972).

Spivack, Bernard, *Shakespeare and the Allegory of Evil* (New York, 1958).

Spurgeon, Caroline, *Shakespeare's Imagery and What It Tells Us* (Cambridge, 1935).

Stewart, J. I. M., *Character and Motive in Shakespeare* (London, 1949); especially regarding the approaches of Bradley and Stoll.

——, 'Shakespeare's Men and their Morals', in *More Talking of Shakespeare* (1959); repr. in Anne Ridler (ed.), *Shakespeare Criticism 1935–1960* (Oxford, 1963) pp. 290–305.

Stoll, Elmer Edgar, *Art and Artifice in Shakespeare* (Cambridge, 1933; New York, 1951).

——, *'Othello': An Historical and Comparative Study* (Minneapolis, 1915).

Traversi, D. A., *An Approach to Shakespeare* (1938; 2nd edn, New York, 1956).

Vyvyan, John, *The Shakespeare Ethic* (London, 1959).

Wain, John (ed.), *'Othello': A Casebook* (London, 1971). See details on p. 88.

Wilson, Edmund, *The Wound and the Bow* (New York, 1941).

The Year's Work in English Studies (English Association and John Murray, London), annual reviews of recent work.

Index to Critics, Authors, Actors

Adamson, J., 22, 24, 41–2, 86–7
Allen, N. B., 12, 79
Aristotle, 77
Auden, W. H., 18, 40, 80

Barthes, R., 51–2
Battenhouse, R. W., 25
Bayley, J., 11–12, 39, 41
Bethell, S. L., 11, 16, 19, 25, 29, 30,
    47, 66
Bodkin, M., 11, 36, 54–5
Bradley, A. C., 9, 10, 11, 16, 18, 24,
    28, 29, 30–1, 32, 37, 38–9, 40, 42,
    44, 57, 62, 64, 85, 87
Brandl, A., 30
Bridges, R., 80
Brock, C., 10
Byrne, M. St C., 87

Campbell, L. B., 42–3
Carroll, L., 82
Chekhov, A. P., 81
Clemen, W., 33, 49
Coghill, N., 33
Coleridge, S. T., 19, 24, 30
Colman, E. A. M., 45
Cornford, F. M., 52
Cushman, L. W., 30

David, R., 24

Eliot, T. S., 20, 38, 40–1, 52, 76
Elliott, G. R., 16, 44, 46, 87
Empson, W., 50

Fiedler, L., 60–1
Foakes, R. A., 44–5
Frazer, Sir J., 52

Freud, S., 34, 36
Frye, N., 9, 10, 16–17, 18, 19, 46–7,
    49–50, 54, 55–8

Gardner, H., 11, 27, 30, 36, 45,
    47–8, 54, 80
Goddard, H., 46
Granville-Barker, H., 11, 16, 37,
    73, 87
Graves, R., 52
Gribble, J., 56

Harrison, G. B., 21
Harrison, J., 52
Heilman, R. B., 49, 86, 87
Heine, H., 28
Hibbard, G., 16, 17–18
Hobbes, T., 73
Holloway, J., 20, 39–40, 41
Hunter, G. K., 22, 23, 24, 36–7

Johnson, Dr S., 15–16, 38
Jones, Eldred, 22–3
Jones, Emrys, 10, 19, 21, 43, 87
Jones, Ernest, 34
Jonson, B., 34, 35–6, 46, 67
Jung, C. G., 52–3, 54

Knight, G. W., 10, 11, 18, 48–9, 67
Knights, L. C., 44–5, 47, 79–80,
    82–3
Kuala, D., 25

Leavis, F. R., 10, 11, 20, 28–9, 31,
    32, 37, 38, 39–40, 41, 42, 44
Lees, F. N., 23
Lessing, G. E., 9
Lewis, C. S., 45

Lodge, D., 13, 58

McAlindon, T., 33
Mack, M., 65–6, 67, 76
Matthews, G. M., 11, 26, 51, 60, 62, 63, 64
Mendonça, B. H. C. de, 32–3
Miller, A., 18, 64, 66–7, 78
Morozov, M., 47
Muir, K., 15, 29, 32, 42–3, 44, 80, 83
Murray, G., 53

Nemirovich-Danchenko, V. I., 43

Olivier, Sir, L., 24, 87
Ostuzhev, A., 43

Pickard-Cambridge, A. W., 52
Pound, E., 45

Rosenberg, M., 31, 32, 86
Ross, L. J., 72–3
Rymer, T., 10, 15–16, 19, 83

Sackton, A. H., 45
Sanders, N., 12, 25, 26, 27, 37, 40
Schücking, L., 27–8, 37
Schlegel, A. W., 9, 36
Shaw, G. B., 70, 76
Shelley, P. B., 50, 56
Scott, W., 35, 53
Scragg, L., 30–2, 54
Sontag, S., 13
Spivack, B., 30, 33
Spurgeon, C., 47
Stewart, J. I. M., 13, 37
Stoll, E. E., 10, 27–8, 29, 30, 37, 42, 49, 54, 80

Traversi, D. A., 41, 42

Vyvyan, J., 43, 73, 87–8

Wain, J., 15, 88
Watson, J., 52
Wilson, E., 35